#BRAINWASHED

A HANDBOOK FOR FREE-THINKING CITIZENS

Barbara Thiele

"Everything can be taken from a man
But one thing:
The last of the human freedoms—
To choose one's attitude
In any given set of circumstances,
To choose one's own way."

from Man's Search for Meaning
Viktor E. Frankl
Holocaust Survivor

Dedication

To my grandchildren, nieces and nephews

Who will inherit both the successes

And failures of my generation.

May you be wiser and ever more successful

Than those who have come before you.

All my love,

Aunt Barbi

"The mind is not a vessel to be filled but a fire to be ignited."

--Plutarch

Table of Contents

How to Use this Book

This book is designed to be a self-help handbook. This means that any one chapter can be read and understood by itself, with little need to have read any of the previous chapters. However, I have tried to organize the book so that the information in each chapter leads logically to the next chapter. Although I do recommend reading the Introduction before reading any of the other chapters, the reader can feel comfortable reading any one chapter that may be of interest to them at any given time and referring back to it in the future.

Although I was not aware of it when writing this book, Chapter One seems to be the most difficult. It attempts to explain the frame of mind needed to use the book and help one's self become or remain a free thinker. The concept of examination of conscience is apparently new to many. I recommend slow-reading this chapter or interrupting the reading of the book after Chapters 3 & 5 to review Chapter 1 on how to implement an examination of conscience in your own life. However, you may choose to skip around and read the chapters that seem most applicable to their own lives before reading other chapters. This book is intended to be kept on the shelf after reading for future reference and to use to refresh your mind regarding the techniques and concepts described.

One awareness that might be helpful is that the information about Maslow's Hierarchy of Needs in Chapter 1 is referred to in Chapters 2 through 4, and the information in Chapter 5 Confirmation Bias is referred to in Chapter 6. So, it should be helpful when reading some chapters if these particular chapters have already been read. I have tried to make it clear when I am referring to these concepts so that if you are feeling confused, you will know where to get the background information you may desire.

I find the information on the human psychological make up fascinating and helpful even after reading about it time and again. I hope you will too. Certainly, I do not keep all this information in my head to recall instantly when needed, which is why I felt a handbook would be appropriate for people like me. I have, however, found that over the years, I am increasingly able to detect propaganda and confirmation bias in my world, and this has led me to feel a greater ability to think freely. I continue to develop this skill, and I hope this book will help you continue your development of this skill too.

Enjoy the book.

Introduction

We, you and I, are the keepers of our democracy. Generation after generation has handed down a strong system of self-governance to their children. Now, it is our turn. However, the playing field has changed—some rules have changed, others abandoned—and the technology and media landscapes present new challenges. Although we all wish to leave our children with a world better, we have neglected cultivating the tools required of democratic citizens to guard our inheritance and pass on the legacy of democracy to our loved ones. That must change if we are to keep our country a free and strong democracy.

This book provides an easy-to-read explanation of the potential for brainwashing in our modern democracies. I'm not talking about the typical idea of brainwashing, which is total control over a person's thinking. Rather, in this book, the discussion is about what I call micro-brainwashing. Micro-brainwashing is the result of the persuasive influences around us that operate to make up our minds for us—to cause us to think the way someone else wants us to think about an issue rather than to exercise our free-thinking skills. My hope is that by using this book, the reader will be able to more consistently think using their own free will and logic. The many methods of micro-brainwashing used in American society and especially in politics, when successful, rob us of our most invaluable tool needed to keep ourselves free. That tool is our ability to think. Clear, logical, independent thinking is essential to a thriving democracy and essential to the real freedom of each individual in a democracy. It is only with the ability and practice of clear, unbiased, logical thinking that each of us is able to be truly free. Although this capability is nearly universal, the actual consistent practice of free thinking is not.

Each of us is responsible for our own critical thinking skills. Critical thinking involves the skills of recognizing fact versus opinion, the ability to determine when an argument does not make sense (fallacy), and the ability to draw intelligent conclusions based on facts, evidence, and good reasoning. Each of us can, if we choose, educate ourselves to practice free thinking. Free thinking is the ability to avoid the influences of propaganda and bias in our decision making. Critical thinking requires some education. It is not always simply common sense. Free thinking starts with awareness, then commitment, and results in the actions needed to free ourselves of the brainwashing we are subjected to in our free society. The focus of this book is on free thinking while bringing in some explanation of key critical thinking skills. There are two basic goals of free thinking: First, prevent emotional reactions from interfering with reason and logic. Second, recognize and prevent outside forces that work to interfere with our ability to use logic and reasoning. This brings me to the point that when we live in a free society, we are exposed to the many acts of freedom practiced by others, some of which will expose us to micro- brainwashing. Knowledge is the best defense, and in a changing world, it is necessary that learning be a way of life.

Too often, and perhaps habitually, many people react to the barrage of information coming at them daily with unspoken compliance—accepting the info-mercials without question. Indeed, it can be overwhelming if we try to take the time to question everything. Part of the problem is time, so we must also learn what must be questioned and analyzed for the sake of protecting our free-thinking independent minds, and what is less consequential. This problem leads to an equally challenging issue. In the technological age we have the freedom to constantly have multiple bits of info streaming to us from multiple sources. Because of this, the inclination may be to develop the habit of unquestioning acceptance or complicity. Most challenging is that this habit feels as if we are ignoring all this input, but in fact, our thinking is being gently molded or remodeled by the information we believe we are ignoring.

This book will teach you to recognize the propaganda to which you are being exposed and which can brainwash those of us who are unaware. This book will help you understand how the human psychological make-up (your psychological make-up) influences what you believe to be true even when good evidence to the contrary exists. This book will explain how basic and not-so-basic human needs influence our beliefs and decisions whether or not there is evidence, and thus, increases our willingness to accept brainwashing. This book will examine social media and how it contributes to brainwashing. It will explain some of the techniques of active measures used by Russia and others in influence campaigns to erode your free thinking. Finally, this book will give you some tools to help you deal with these challenges. The treatment of each of these issues is not intended to be comprehensive. Instead, this book is intended to be useful in scope and size. My hope is that you will keep this book as an easy-to-use-as-needed reference. Listed at the back are some resources that offer more in-depth understanding of what is presented here.

I hope you will find this handbook helpful in your effort to be a free-thinking, contributing citizen of a democracy. In America we believe that freedom is a right and fight fiercely to protect our physical freedoms. The time has come when we must fight just as fiercely to protect the freedom of our thoughts. Unlike physical freedom, free thinking must be learned and cultivated and passed on to our children. Free thinking is not free.

My hope is that my book will help you become free of brainwashing and become the free-thinking individual you were meant to be.

{ 12 }

Chapter 1

The Importance of Self-Awareness –
Examination of Conscience & Maslow's Needs

In his 1983 book *Lost in the Cosmos*, Walker Percy asks this question: "Why is it possible to learn more in ten minutes about Crab Nebula in Taurus, which is 6,000 light-years away, than you presently know about yourself, even though you've been stuck with yourself all your life" and "despite 10,000 self-help books, 100,000 psychotherapists, and 100 million fundamentalist Christians."

We must learn the practice of examination of conscience. An examination of conscience is a review of ones' past thoughts, words, actions, reactions and omissions for the purpose of recognizing whether we are living the way we believe we should be living. In essence, it is a close look at ourselves in an effort to improve and build upon what we already love about who we are. Examination of conscience can use standards and values we choose or standards and values we learn from others such as parents, churches, and educational endeavors, etc.

I was fortunate to grow up in a home with loving parents who wanted the very best for their kids. Dad sent his first four kids to religious school, and Mom stayed home to keep a clean, orderly home and make sure the kids not only got to after-school events, but also got the guidance needed to live up to our potential. Despite their very best efforts, each of us has a few hang-ups, some lack of confidence here or a bit of selfishness there, etc. You know, the little aspects of personality that just aren't perfect and sometimes get in the way of our pursuit of healthy living and right thinking. Of the many things I am thankful for in my upbringing, learning how to do an examination of conscience is one of the top on my list. My religious school taught the practice of regularly assessing whether we were living according to our values in the actions of our everyday lives. An honest self-awareness was believed to be an important part of a values-driven life.

Nurturing Examination of Conscience

Developing free thinking starts with self-awareness and examination of conscience. If we are to guard our democratic heritage, we must first accept our responsibility to ourselves. The challenge we humans face of thinking independently (or working toward increased independent thought) first arises from our basic psychological framework. Much of this framework is likely based on the mix of environmental conditions an individual has dealt with throughout his/her life. So, it is not the same for every individual. Still, there are aspects of human psychology that we share in common to one degree or another. The differences may be from the nurture (or lack of nurture) we have received as we passed through the various stages of life. Because of this, readers are encouraged to do an examination of conscience, an exploration of one's personal attitudes and emotional reactions to the world and information encountered in their daily lives. How have the significant people and experiences in your life affected your perspectives and emotions? How do impactful relationships and experiences affect your decision-making?

In practicing self-awareness (for the purpose of free thinking), the goal is for people to develop an increasingly greater understanding of themselves and the quick, automatic responses they bring to everyday experiences. Many people find writing a journal or diary to be helpful in this. Others simply practice looking inward throughout the day or before drifting to sleep—recognizing both their emotional and mental reactions to the circumstances of their day. Most importantly, this examination of conscience or reflection must include an exercise of free will. To be effective, it must include your own personal decision about whether you choose to accept your reflexive emotional and mental reactions as a positive or negative influence in your life and your decision-making. If positive, keep those reactions. If negative, choose to change those reactions that do not serve your free-thinking. How? By continuing to recognize when you react negatively and using your conscience to eventually overcome this negative reaction, replacing it with a more positive emotional and/or mental reaction. Some people may use prayer, meditation, positive affirmation (self-talk) or other forms of mindfulness to help overcome the reflexive responses they find to be harmful to their free-thinking abilities. Find what works for you and be diligent. It takes time, but consistent effort will pay off. Use this book to help you recognize what you might choose to change. (It is so great to live in a country where we are free to choose.)

An Examination of Conscience Example

A personal example included recognizing an influence I grew up with and how it could impact me in my everyday life. At one point in my early twenties, I heard my father talking with my nephew about an activity Doug was having fun pursuing. Dad was questioning Doug with, "Now, how could you have done that better?" Well now, that seems like constructive Grandpa questioning, but it occurred to me that my father, Grandpa, had failed to say anything positive about Doug's efforts when beginning the conversation. This may seem inconsequential, but upon examining this seemingly trivial experience, I realized two things. First, Dad had implied that Doug's efforts were not good enough. Think about how an impressionable, sensitive twelve-year-old's feelings of confidence would be dashed by this implication. Ouch! Second, if this was how I was raised (as it likely was) no wonder I so often had feelings of self-doubt.

Ah, hah! The unexplained lack of self-confidence I often felt may have come from Dad— bless his heart, who was only trying to help me be a better person. Now, recognizing this, I could understand that this negative emotional reaction (self-doubt) had been learned. It was not a reasonable reaction, but it was often automatic. Such feelings or reactions would undermine my confidence in my ability to think for myself. However, using my rational free will, I could gradually overcome it. Believe me, it wasn't easy, because any time someone challenged me, I tended to be overcome with self-doubt. I fought the reaction with positive self-talk and by reflecting on the many situations in which my ideas had worked or been validated in some way. However, I always re-evaluated the ideas challenged to make sure I was making decisions based on reason rather than emotional reaction. I had to be open-minded to the possibility somebody had a better idea than mine, but I didn't have to feel bad or have self-doubt.

By teaching myself to react with reason instead of emotion, I could free my mind to think more clearly without allowing someone else to instill their ideas into my brain. I could evaluate others' ideas first before choosing to either accept or disregard them. This is the 1st goal of free thinking— the ability to prevent our learned emotional reactions from interfering with our reason and our ability to draw logical conclusions. The 2nd goal is to recognize the forces around us that can work to interfere with our free-thinking and then prevent such interference. Recognition of these forces is the initial step required.

Take some time to examine a recent emotional reaction of your own. Do you let that emotion determine your behavior and decision-making, or are you able to recognize that your emotional reaction may not be helpful in making a rational decision? Are you able to think freely without or despite the influence of your emotion? Please note, emotions are not bad. They just tend to confuse and hinder our reasoning. I'm not suggesting you try to turn off your emotions. Many emotions—love, fear, empathy, etc.—are necessary for individual health and happiness. I am urging that you learn to recognize when an emotion or reaction is getting in the way of logical thinking. The beauty of life is deeply connected not only to our emotions but also to our ability to reason. Learning to choose whether emotion or reason is the best response for any given situation (or to balance these mental giants) are the lessons of everyone's lifetime. It takes repeated practice to hone this skill. Be persistent and there will be payoffs.

Maslow's Hierarchy of Needs

Recognizing our basic needs as humans is helpful in assessing how personal motivation or need fulfillment will affect our perspective and emotional reactions. For this, a basic understanding of Maslow's Hierarchy of Needs should be considered. Abraham Maslow, an American psychologist, first proposed his "Theory of Human Motivation" in 1943 and later more fully developed it in his 1954 book *Motivation and Personality*. His theories parallel many other theories of human developmental psychology and continue to be used widely in analyzing human motivation and mental health.[1]

The needs Maslow proposed as basic to all humans are often presented in a pyramid to show that those at the base are foundational. This implies that until lower needs are fulfilled, higher needs will be more difficult to meet and perhaps less motivating. However, later studies resulted in the conclusion that higher needs can be motivating even when lower needs are not fully met. "Maslow noted that the order of needs may be flexible based on external circumstances or individual differences."[2] Each of us may value and be motivated by each need in varying degrees depending upon factors in our personality as well as factors in our environment. In 1987, Maslow further pointed out that most behavior is multi-motivated. Several or even all the needs may be at play to varying degrees in motivating human behavior.[3]

In the 1970s Maslow expanded his basic 5-stage model to 8 stages, and we will examine only the later model to avoid redundancy. At the base of the 8-stage model are four stages considered deficiency needs. The upper four levels are considered growth needs. Deficiency or deficit needs motivate people primarily when we are deprived. When a deficit need is met, it will diminish or perhaps even go away as a motivator. On the other hand, "growth needs continue to be felt and may even become stronger once they are engaged."[4]

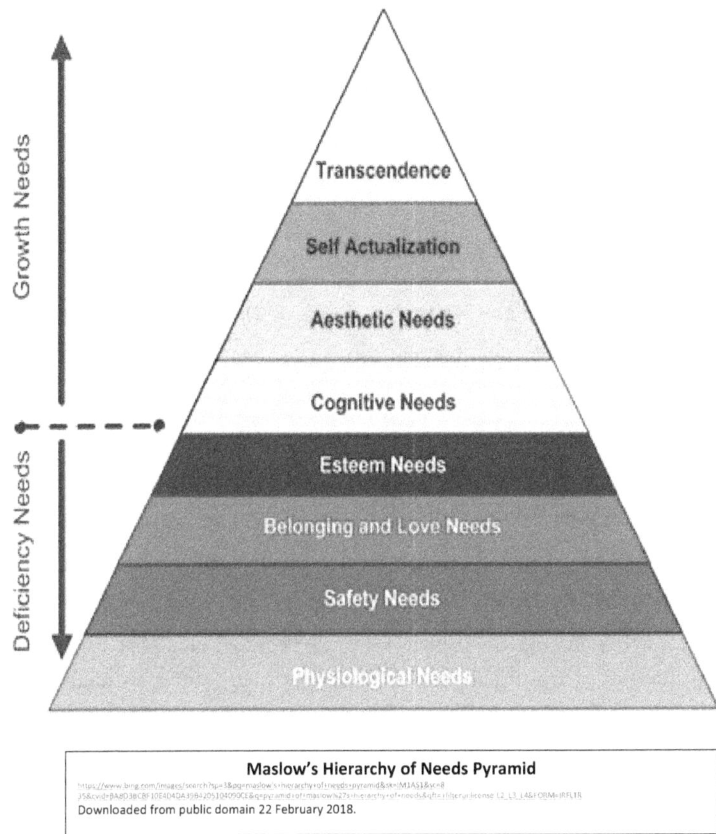

Maslow's Hierarchy of Needs Pyramid

Maslow's Deficit Needs

Level 1: Physiological Needs—The physiological needs include air, water, food, warmth, shelter, sex and sleep. These are the basics of both physiological and psychological health. If one of these is unsatisfied or inconsistently satisfied, it could affect our motivations. This is true of each level.

Level 2: Safety Needs—The second level, safety, includes protections from the elements and feelings of security, order, and stability. Lack of any of these is temporarily tolerable, unlike level one. However, the lack of one of these needs is only temporarily okay. Over time, the need for feeling safe becomes necessary to flourish and be able to use opportunities to their best advantage. Without security and stability, high levels of distraction and feelings of uncertainty interfere with the normal function of the brain.

Level 3: Love and Belonging Needs—includes friendship, intimacy, trust, acceptance, receiving and giving affection and love. It also includes affiliating or being part of a group (family, friends, work colleagues, community groups, church, etc.) Note that this need level includes both giving to and receiving from others. Lacking any of these can be tolerated for a time, but if missing for too long, these needs will manifest themselves in our motivation and drive. This need level is significant and is part of what drives the "tribalism" we currently see in our politics. I will discuss this more in the chapter titled "Herd Instinct," and there are several books that devote themselves to this concept and how it is affecting our democracy; some are listed in the works consulted section of this book.

Level 4: Esteem—The final deficit needs are for esteem. Maslow classified these into two categories. First is esteem for oneself: dignity, independence, achievement, and mastery. Second is desire for reputation or esteem from others. For example: respect, status, and prestige. To be fulfilled, this level is dependent, in part, on others. Because of this, the need for esteem can be noticed in the conversations we hear in social settings. When people say something to impress others, they are trying to fulfill their need for esteem. This need, like need #3, is a strong driver of political and social opinions. It should be examined closely within one's self. When this need is present, it tends to limit our willingness to be free thinkers. The need for esteem may make us unwilling to go against the tide when our own thinking conflicts with that of people whose opinions we value and whose acceptance we may crave. Rather than risk ridicule or getting a cold-shoulder from friends or family, we may remain silent. We may even change our mind to insure we stay on the good side of those we esteem. We all want respect and to be seen as worthy by others.

Maslow's Growth Needs

The growth needs (levels 5-8) are categorized as cognitive, aesthetic, self-actualization, and transcendence. I would argue that some people (not all or most) are only motivated by growth needs if the needs are learned or nurtured, or if the need is valued for the fulfillment of a deficit need. Most people will understand how deficit needs can and do motivate them. However, when examining the growth needs, some people will see them as luxuries from which people can pick and choose freely. Many sayings, parables, and folktales suggest this. "Business before pleasure" is a classic that basically conveys the message, "Take care of your deficit needs, and only then concern yourself with your growth needs."

Be that as it may, many will see aspects of these needs as motivating factors in their lives. It is helpful to acknowledge that growth needs are very strong motivating factors in some, but less motivating in others. And again, the degree of motivating influence may be determined by environmental circumstances or learned values. For example, if you are raised in a home where music or art is valued, that growth need may become highly motivating to you. Some might also argue that the more civilized or advanced a society, the more motivating and valued growth needs become. I believe there is evidence for this.

Level 5: Cognitive Needs—Knowledge, understanding, curiosity, exploration and the need for meaning is encouraged in modern civilized society via public education, which is almost universally seen as a right rather than a privilege. This need can easily be linked to the evolutionary survival of humans as well. Propaganda, which is discussed in detail in chapter 3, attempts to manipulate the motivators this need creates. Propaganda uses fear of losing one or more deficit needs to convince people to believe untruths and twisted truths, and then to shut down curiosity, exploration and other cognitive needs because the propagandist has convinced us that all the knowledge and understanding needed has been provided. This is where free thinking can be shut down without a person's awareness unless one is willing to work at recognizing propaganda and challenging it. These skills will be explained in the chapter on propaganda.

Level 6: Aesthetic Needs or the appreciation and search for beauty, has become celebrated in America's National Endowment for the Arts. It's value to people can also be measured by the amount of money spent by theater, movie and concert goers as well as home decorators and others making a living creating beauty. Most of us know at least one person who enjoys spending money on things that have no value other than their beauty and the feeling of joy such beauty brings to them. Many of these types of people bring great joy to others because they seem to be able to readily celebrate the beauty in the world around them, and they pass this feeling of celebration and joy to those they meet and touch.

Level 7: Self-actualization is the realizing of personal potential through self-fulfillment, personal growth, and peak experience, religious faith, scientific understanding, aesthetic and mystical experiences, etc. According to SimplePsychology.com, "As each individual is unique, the motivation for self-actualization leads people in different directions." Perhaps self-actualization can be explained as the need to achieve personal goals and to move on from one goal to the next throughout our lives. Again, some are more motivated than others in this area of growth. It seems some people always have a new goal to work towards, whereas others find contentment in having achieved their current situation and so have no need to find yet another goal. I believe both types of persons have lessons we can all learn.

Level 8: Transcendence Needs are values that go beyond the previous seven need levels. These needs drive motivation for many, but not all people. Such values include spiritual experiences, the need to feel a relationship with a spiritual entity, and the need to feel you are living up to the standards of a higher being that goes beyond the full understanding of humans. This legitimate need can be particularly dangerous to free thinking because people are often willing to deny logic in the name of some higher being whose ability to reason is thought to be beyond human comprehension. I am not denying the existence of God, but faith should not be used as an excuse to avoid the use of logic. A dilemma is created when logic is abandoned. The abandonment of logic has led humankind to many perplexing challenges throughout history. Some have led to brutal and cruel behavior. Furthermore, I don't deny transcendental experiences (Indeed, I have always believed they do occur.) However, I believe my mother's dictum does not contradict transcendence. Mom proclaimed, "God gave us a brain because God intended us to use it." And Grandma would say, "Honey-child, use your gifts." The point is that believing in a higher power does not change the fact that the gift of logic is part of the foundation of human progress and, as such, should be turned to for answers and decisions whenever possible.

Applying Maslow's Needs

Looking at Maslow's Basic Needs, it isn't hard to extrapolate that people who feel economically threatened, i.e. facing a possible layoff or loss of job, would be highly motivated. I remember when I was just out of college and without a job how much anxiety I felt wondering how I would pay my way. How could I ask my parents for help when they had been helping me get my education? Without a sufficient income, we all face basic need insecurity. That insecurity is a vulnerability for politicians and sometimes advertisers to take advantage of and exploit. Politicians will try to convince you they can do what is needed to give us economic security. In a democracy where capitalism is practiced, the truth is that individual politicians can have only a small effect on the economic security of individuals, but of course, political adds will try to convince voters otherwise. Overstating one's personal ability to "fix the economy" and sway others to agree to one's ideas is another hallmark of political mumbo-jumbo. Beware! Because most advertising is expensive, and therefore quick and flashy, many propaganda techniques will be used including blame and disparagement, but rarely will a thorough discussion of the facts and economic theories be put forth. It is worth noting that many voters are unwilling to consider in-depth analyses of issues, so many politicians don't feel it is worth their time. Instead, they use propaganda and advertising techniques to win votes. If we are truly interested in being free-thinkers, we must demand in-depth analyses, and we must be willing to pay careful attention when it is presented. We may even have to do the analyses ourselves.

With the real threat of terrorism, cyber-crime, and identity theft now a part of everyday life, appealing to our need for security, both personal and national, has become an almost daily assault on our sensibilities and logical reasoning. A free thinker will not let these or any fear disengage his/her logic and reasoning ability.

Unfortunately, this type of propaganda is quite often prejudicial or, in the extreme, racist. The reality of crime and terrorism plays up our fears, making us more vulnerable and receptive to micro-brainwashing.

Because we have a legitimate and reasonable fear, prejudicial assertions appear to be reasonable, but reasonable fear does not equal reasonable prejudice. When we go beyond our emotional reactions, and exercise careful observation of facts, the belief that a prejudice is legitimate because a fear is legitimate often proves untrue. This is the argument against racial profiling, which lumps all people of one race into the category of criminals and therefore to be treated as criminals, a clearly unreasonable prejudice. That is not to say it is unreasonable to be suspicious of a person in a dark alley at 1 AM—but it is the environment that gives reason for suspicion—not the person's race. By the way, why are you in the dark alley at 1 AM? I'm sure you have a good reason to be there—Right? Maintaining a clear understanding of how fear and prejudice differ is important to maintaining the ability to be a free-thinker. Free thinkers will avoid jumping on this brainwashed bandwagon just because of the appearance of truth and reasonableness.

Probably the most powerful of Maslow's deficit needs are at level 3— love and belonging. Approval and acceptance from our friends and the groups we associate or identify with is a powerful driver of motivation. I think we can all relate to this. It is at this level many of us, unwittingly, are most vulnerable. Fear of rejection by those we love or have friendships with drives us to say and do things daily. Indeed, the fact that we humans frequently say and do things just for the positive impression we think we will make on others is clearly a result of our motivation to be accepted by those we care about. Political parties are national groups we choose to associate with— sometimes based on careful analysis of what the party stands for, but more often based on stereotypes of the party we have heard from other groups we belong to such as family, friends, and work colleagues, or the party itself. Identity politics works because we want to belong.

Most of us belong to several groups until one of our groups alienates another, then we recoil as well. Within the two-party system of America there are many groups people choose to identify with: gun owners, right-to-lifers, White middle class, Black lives matter, religious groups, civil rights groups, etc., etc. If a cause or group is seen as rejecting one or more of the groups a person identifies or sympathizes with, an emotional reaction may call into question the rightfulness of the threatening cause or group. That emotional reaction may drown out the logical reasons for the threatening group's or cause's existence. When this happens, our reasoning fails us and prejudices drive our behavior and attitudes. Prejudices shut down logical thinking, create animosity and suspicion, and keep our country divided. The more appropriate response is to logically assess the reasons for the existence of each group/cause and then to determine to what extent each has reasonable positions. We can also recognize that each may go too far in one or more of their positions. From here, we can determine if there are commonalities and whether conflicting groups/causes can be supported reasonably or whether compromise is possible.

Clashes between the Black Lives Matter groups and law and order groups can serve as an example. In this case, ironically, each group shares the same goal: legal protections of citizens' rights. However, the emotional reactions we have for those in the other group may reflect our prejudices, instead of our reasoning. Law and order supporters are generally white and perhaps fearful of blacks on dark streets in the middle of the night. They want protection. Blacks and their supporters are fearful of people wearing uniforms and abusing their legal authority, many of whom are white, but not all. They want protection. Both want the justice system to be fair, but each may see the same situations differently. Reasoning should lead us to see that we are fighting for the same thing, but our emotions lead us to feel we are fighting each other. What a waste of energy. We are all Americans! Let's be logical and work together to solve a problem that threatens us all. Fighting each other simply makes problems more difficult to solve. We can disagree on the methods used to insist on law and order, but there is no reason to vilify each other, and working together is more likely to get the problems solved sooner.   (Please see the section on vilification propaganda in Chapter 3 Propaganda.)

Summary

There are many psychological needs that drive human behavior, reactions, and thinking. If we are to be able to think freely, we must be aware of these psychological needs and take the reins they have on our thinking into our conscious hands. We must rein in our emotional and automatic reactions to avoid undermining our logic and our ability to step back and analyze what is in front of us. Not doing so will result in being brainwashed as we give in to human nature and psychological needs that press us into illogical thinking. Keep in mind, what is natural is not always logical, and it takes effort to avoid the micro-brainwashing that may result.

Chapter 2

How Propaganda Became a Problem in America

As a child in the 1960s, I watched black and white television with only three news channels to choose from: ABC, NBC, and CBS. As I recall, all three channels started at 6 PM and ended 30 minutes later. I guess if you wanted in-depth analyses, you had to subscribe to a major newspaper. Dad bought the LA Times, the San Francisco Chronicle, and the local Times Delta. Watching the news in my house was like a religion. Dad never missed it, so neither did we kids. He used to admonish us that we should read the newspapers and know what was going on in the world, so I did. Because of this, I was a news junkie by the age of ten. I grew up watching the Vietnam War, the assassination of John F. Kennedy, the Civil Rights Movement, and anti-war protests from the comfort of my living room couch. Perhaps I should thank my lucky stars such turmoil and tragedy were only visible for thirty minutes a day. After the news, shows like *Lassie* and *Leave it to Beaver* schooled me in how the world was supposed to be. The changes in our television news and our news consumption has had profound effects on our country, but even more profound effects have been created by television advertising and the use of sly propaganda techniques that constantly bombard us with desensitizing persuasion.

America is experiencing what I will call a reasoning crisis due in large part to this propaganda, and this crisis is destroying our democracy as well as our government. This crisis did not suddenly appear in the 21st century but has crept slowly and insidiously into our culture over the course of the 20th century despite our country's impressive gains in education. The importance of this to our freedom and democracy is well-explained in Al Gore's *The Assault on Reason.*

Mr. Gore notes that the Founding Fathers intended that "the only legitimate source of power in America was to be the consent of the governed, wealth was not to be bartered for political power." He asserts,

> "If the reasoning process is corrupted by money and deception then the consent of the governed is based on false premises, and any power thus derived is inherently counterfeit and unjust. If the consent of the governed is extorted through the manipulation of mass fears…democracy is impoverished."[5]

Several changes in our society have caused mass fear and propaganda to become problematic in our country, and wealth is a part of that problem. I am not asserting that wealth is a bad thing, but that it can be and is, at times, used to achieve bad goals; and when used for such purposes, it must be checked (regulated) to protect the Constitutional rights of all citizens. Regulation has only recently become a dirty word in the political arena, seen as diminishing freedoms and economic opportunity. I argue that democracy and capitalism work well only if government can find the proper balance between regulation to protect the rights of citizens (from capitalist greed and lack of moral compass) and lack of regulation to promote personal liberty and our capitalist economy. It is a delicate balance, but to protect democracy, it must be achieved, and citizens must be able to come to well-reasoned conclusions as to where the logical balance points within our system are to be established. So, it is critical that we identify the causes of our reasoning crisis and solve the problem.

Some Causes of America's Reasoning Crises

1. News Media Changes & Personal Choices

Our reasoning crisis stems from the growth of five changes in our society. Some of these changes have to do with the expansion of the news media, but some have to do with personal choices. First, cable television media channels are increasingly polarized and biased, emphasizing their preferred view of issues. Of course, our First Amendment protects their right to do so. (For more information on this problem see chapter 7 on the news media.) On the other hand, most people, if they watch news at all, watch the same programs day in and day out, so they are likely to receive prejudicial perspectives repeatedly. Repetition is a strong propaganda tool and will be discussed in Chapter 3: Propaganda: Recognizing the Basics. By making the personal choice to constantly watch biased news commentary, we promote in ourselves that same bias. Part of the solution is simply to deliberately watch a variety of news shows with different prejudices throughout the week. Easily said, not as easily done, because we want to be in our comfort zone, especially when snuggled on the couch in front of the T.V. However, it is only when we step out of our comfort zones that we learn anything new, and all citizens in a democracy contribute most when they are engaged in learning more about themselves and their country. Another problem is simply time. Who has enough time to watch two or three news programs every evening. A solution to this is to alternate the news programs you choose to watch throughout the week.

Why is it our major news programs no longer present information from unbiased perspectives? Follow the money. First, it is so expensive to own and operate a television news program that, except for the Public Broadcasting Service, many are owned by wealthy fat cats with their own biased agenda. Note that some, not all, newspapers are victim to this situation as well, and the result is similar. The news presented by these sources is infused with bias and propaganda. It's helpful to find out who owns the news media from which you are getting information. It is also helpful to know how they vet or don't vet the information they pass on to us. Refer to Chapter 7: Real News, Fake News, or Alternative Facts for help with determining trustworthy news sources. But, most importantly, it is important to recognize when bias and propaganda is presented.

2. Trustworthy News Organizations' Lack of Financial Support from Citizenry

A second cause of our reasoning crisis is our unwillingness or lack of interest in reading newspapers. By and large, newspapers are still the most trustworthy sources of news. Larger newspapers, specifically those at the state level of circulation, usually present opposing views over time, but not always side by side, which would be more helpful. Many offer their readers in-depth coverage of current events and issues. Best of all, to some extent, they point out what is fact, allegation, and opinion by the section and subtitles used. It is still our job, however, to figure out what is fact and opinion within newspaper articles. Chapter 7 helps the reader with this skill. Many television news outlets blur the distinction between these three critical categories: fact, opinion, and allegation. Also, newspapers let readers weigh in with their views, promoting a dialogue of sorts for open-minded, free-thinking individuals willing to consider many sides of an issue before jumping to a conclusion. Many offer online subscriptions, and they are well worth the cost. If read regularly, facts and opinions can be weighed, analyzed, further investigated (highly recommended), and used to make informed decisions.

3. Deregulation and Owners' Political Agendas

A third cause of America's reasoning crisis is related to the second. As the rich take over news disseminating organizations, they lobby effectively for deregulation and unfettered ability to promote their agendas. This, of course, receives little news coverage to avoid public outcry, and often it is done in the name of "free speech," which being an emotionally charged phrase, weakens our brains reasoning capacity to recognize all the logical reasons deregulation may not be in the best interest of our citizens. So, in recent years media owners and investors have been quite successful in changing the media rules so that (among other rules) the requirement to present all sides of an issue has been dropped. Some programs try to present both sides, others give lip-service to presenting both sides but emphasize one side while denigrating the other. More on this in Chapter Seven.

Furthermore, monopoly media holdings are no longer seen as the threat they really are to democracy. The Federal Communications Commission is influenced by the politics of the day in recent years and operates with little attention to the public interest beyond the interest of the dollar. Big money will control our country's destiny unless enough un-brainwashed and watchful citizens speak out and vote wisely. If the wealthy elite have too much control, America will be an oligarchy instead of a democracy, much like Russia and other pseudo-democracies that have elections with very little meaning or impact on the government. Free-thinking citizens taking an active role in their democracy is the prevention for this very real threat.

4. Simplistic Thinking and Lack of Imagination

The fourth cause is summed up in this quote from Ralph Waldo Emerson: "A foolish consistency is the hobgoblin of little minds...." Our reasoning crisis stems from the devotion of our own little minds to interpret our constitutional ideals with foolish simplistic consistency. The Founding Fathers wisely attempted to write our Constitution in general terms so that its application could evolve with the ever-changing times. Perhaps they recognized that to be too specific would limit the usefulness of the document. Unfortunately, little minds apply "all or nothing" error to our Constitution. Many are unable to recognize that logical reasoning leads us to know that there will be logical exceptions to many rules. For instance, many of us assume that any limit on free speech is unconstitutional. The result is the implementation of free speech unreasonably. Many believe, erroneously, that we must protect all free speech or risk having no free speech at all. This simple-minded approach has resulted in media mega-monopolies and the deluge of propaganda they disseminate. That is not to say the media mega-monopolies don't have some value; they do. It is to say that citizens will be brainwashed if they do not exercise their free-thinking skills. We have a duty and responsibility to be wise users of all our media sources, whatever they may be, and to demand reasonable and wisely written regulations.

There are examples of when free speech is justifiably limited, such as in laws against defamation of character. The argument for this legal constraint is the constitutional right to liberty and the pursuit of happiness. If one's character is tarnished by malicious lies or truth-twisting, one's life will have both its liberty and happiness diminished unconstitutionally. The logical conclusion is that to the degree one's person's right to free speech diminishes another person's constitutional rights, reasonable limitations must be imposed. Thus, the Supreme Court has done just that.

This is not to say that the Supreme Court is always right. The Supreme Court's logic in asserting that the giving of money is a form of free speech and, therefore, cannot be regulated seems unreasonable. Since all citizens do not have the same amount of money and do not have equal opportunity to use money to voice their opinions, it seems this ruling redistributes the power of free speech to the advantage of the wealthy. Furthermore, I would argue that a reasonable case can be made for the regulation or limitation of propaganda in both our news media and our political campaigns despite our right to free speech. Imagine how helpful it would be if all advertising was required to print at the bottom what types of propaganda were used in the ad? I think this would be just as reasonable as having disclaimers beneath smoking ads indicating the surgeon general has determined that cigarettes cause cancer.

Citizens need to imagine how we could better use our Constitution to improve our country and advance civilization. We must not let ourselves be stuck in the 18th century.

5. Our Inability to Recognize Propaganda and Defend Ourselves

The inability of so many people to recognize propaganda contributes immensely to the reasoning crisis with which we are afflicted. Clearly, if one is not aware of the techniques being used to influence him or her, one cannot be expected to be able to prevent the brainwashing results such techniques are intended to have. Free thinking must start with an ability to see when arguments for or against something are based in propaganda instead of logical reasoning. Propaganda techniques are a powerful tool in the arsenal of advertisers and politicians, and we must develop our own arsenal of logical and free-thinking abilities to defend against the unfair advantage it gives to those who use propaganda to drumroll us into submitting to their whims.

> "If the reasoning process is corrupted by money
> and deception [propaganda] then the consent of the

> governed is based on false premises, and any power thus
> derived is inherently counterfeit and unjust."[6]

Let's consider how this assertion might play out in our society. Both money and propaganda work, often together, to buy or win votes. In the case of propaganda, which we will look at carefully in the next chapter, votes are won unfairly by selling lies or twisted truths to the voters. Although voters legitimately choose a candidate, it can be argued the winner of an election who did so by deception (propaganda) is not a legitimate winner. (Note: Large amounts of money are used to buy television and social media propaganda to win votes.) Since he/she has deceived voters, he/she has unfairly won their votes. If the process is not fair, the outcome is not fair. The power this person has been given by the voters is counterfeit because it was won unfairly, using deception and other means that avoid or obscure the truth. The person winning power this way is by definition an unjust leader, meaning he/she has not won the approval of the voters based on truth. For a democracy to have integrity or be a true democracy, the voters must be able to vote based on true information and leaders must be elected based on the truth of their ideas, promises, and commitments. Propaganda should play no role whatsoever.

Conclusion

Currently, in the American system, there is no way to prevent the use of money and propaganda to mislead or misinform the public. There is no Constitutional limit on its use. In fact, in the Supreme Court ruling frequently referred to as the Citizens United case, one theory of free speech is allowed to protect the use of money and propaganda in public discourse. The validity of the argument and decision made in this case deserves close examination by all citizens because our only recourse, if we disagree with this perspective, is to create laws and regulations that will correct the misinterpretation. Citizens will have to force a Constitutional amendment if United States legislators will not fix the problem. A reminder: Our Supreme Court is only supposed to interpret the current laws; our legislators create and modify them.

Our media is charged with the task of discerning and disseminating the truth and unmasking falsehood, exaggeration, and misleading information. Some news providers take great pride in providing this service while others seem to deliberately participate in promoting lies and misleading information as they pursue an agenda that goes beyond providing news and promotes their own political goals. Perhaps our founding fathers believed people of integrity and honesty would be more appealing to voters, but the strength of marketing techniques and the power of big money is far too enormous in today's world to be outgunned by honesty and integrity on a consistent basis. This is a BIG problem. Certainly, honesty and integrity do win sometimes, but it only takes a few corrupt and dishonest people in leadership positions to mess up the system and steer us toward calamity. Our checks and balances are helpful, but an informed citizenry is a more potent and effective check on unjust and corruptly held power within our system of government. And it is likely that informed citizens are the only effective check on misguided rulings of the Supreme Court, albeit one that takes an enormous effort.

Ultimately, we the citizens of this great nation must know and demand the truth to be able to protect our precious democracy. In order to do this, we must be able to protect ourselves from the influence of propaganda and other aspects of our society that undermine our free thinking.

Chapter 3

Propaganda: Recognizing the Basics

If I use this product, my hair will grow thicker; if I buy this product, I will be handsome and attractive to women; if I take this product, I will live to be 100; and if I vote for this candidate, all the evils of the world will be corrected. The world of advertising and politics constantly tries to fill our heads with false hope and the improbable. Although hope is a very positive and desirable emotion, it must be tempered with realism, fact, and logic. Propaganda and emotional filters can reduce our ability to balance hope with fact and logic.

A Brief History of Propaganda in America

Propaganda, according to Merriam-Webster, is "ideas or statements that are often false or exaggerated and that are spread in order to help a cause [or damage an opposing cause], a political leader, government, etc."

Americans and most, if not all, Westernized cultures are inundated with the propaganda of marketing. The use of propaganda in American culture became anathema after WWI when citizens were made aware of how the Allied countries, especially the United States and Great Britain, used propaganda to promote falsehoods that resulted in increased support for the war among the civilian population. Americans were outraged at the manipulation they belatedly realized had been used to mold public opinion. Ironically, similar manipulation led Americans into the Iraq war almost a century later. Most Americans now recognize that there were no weapons of mass destruction and that Iraq was not working with Al-Qaeda, yet propaganda continues to sway public opinion on other critical issues of our time. Are we surrendering our reasoning capability and allowing ourselves to be brainwashed? I hope not. In fact, the writing of this book demonstrates my trust that many Americans simply have not been taught to recognize falsehood and propaganda. This chapter will focus on identifying marketing propaganda, which is used both in business and politics.

How Television Propaganda Exerts Social Control

Since the 1960s our television programming has been funded by business interests selling us their goods and services. They use subtle and not so subtle marketing schemes. Many television marketing techniques are essentially propaganda— exaggerated and sometimes false claims to sell a product or service (the cause). Since we are barraged by it whenever we sit in front of a T.V., many of us become desensitized to the manipulative and false nature of these techniques. Most of us watch television for entertainment, and we are not concerned that there are salesmen and politicians sneaking into our homes while we relax, curled up on our sofas with chips and beer or wine and cheese or prepackaged, frozen dinners or whatever. Perhaps we are tired and we just want to enjoy a show. So, when the ads hit us, our cranial defense systems (brains) are not engaged for self-defense. The mute button is one possible savior, but the pictures and graphics can speak a thousand words. It may not be a serious problem if we put on a few pounds because we are convinced Betty Crocker's fudge brownies will bring us joy in our relationships, but when the politicians' marketing crews begin buying our vote unchallenged, our free thinking is the victim of our habit of passive watching. They don't call it the boob-tube for nothing.

It is essential, however, to recognize the techniques themselves and then how we react to them emotionally so that we can insulate our minds and prevent the micro-brainwashing these techniques are intended to perpetrate upon us while we passively enjoy our favorite T.V. shows. One reason we need these skills is that we cannot take the pictures off the screen. Muting and closing your eyes would likely only be a great annoyance, and the internet and social media are riddled with the same propagandistic advertising. Hence, it is essential we examine propaganda and marketing techniques carefully with the goal of self-protection and development of free thinking. We will start with the easiest and most obvious propaganda/marketing techniques and work to the more subtle and difficult to guard ourselves against. However, it bears repeating that any of these techniques can begin to brainwash us if we do not actively fight them with reason.

REPETITION as Propaganda

Repetition is one of the most powerful tools in the persuasive toolbox of propaganda. It has been said that if you repeat something often enough, people will believe it. Teachers know that repetition is a very powerful teaching tool, and good teachers use it. To the wise listener, it is easy to detect this in the speeches of most politicians. Slogans are repeated endlessly as are arguments and talking points. It is a very persuasive tool.

Why is it such a simple technique can overpower our logic? I'll leave that for psychologists to explain in depth, but my theory is that people become desensitized when something is repeated. Our conscious minds stop paying attention to it, but our sub-conscious minds still hear it. Every time it is heard by the sub-conscious, it is etched or re-etched into a place in our brain without any questioning or doubt expressed. Lacking the conscious expression of doubt, people begin to accept what has been repeated as fact. My solution is to express my doubts silently to myself when I first hear something of which I am not sure, no matter whether I trust the source from which I am hearing it or not. (After all, everyone makes mistakes.) After that, I continue this until when I hear the repetition, my brain goes on auto-pilot with the doubt. If the time comes when I have proof of the truth, I correct my ideas about it. You will see why practicing this skill is essential when you read chapter 5 "Confirmation Bias." Research has proven that once we believe something, it is very hard to correct that belief even if the evidence is against it.

NAME-CALLING Propaganda

Another easy-to-recognize technique that is still considered childish by most and beneath people of integrity has recently become fashionable. Name-calling can be used to belittle, demonize, or—most dangerously—dehumanize. The act of dehumanizing other human beings is so dangerous because psychologically it gives the person buying into the dehumanizing the belief that they have the right to exercise all manner of inhumane treatment upon their victims. Thus, many atrocities have been perpetrated on our brothers and sisters in the belief that these people were somehow less than ourselves and therefore, less than human. Obvious examples include slavery, the holocaust, witch-burning, the Crusades, and recently the beheadings and other acts of violence perpetrated by ISIS, the Islamic State. To ISIS most Westerners are labeled infidels, meaning persons who do not believe in what ISIS believes in, and so must be eradicated to protect the pure of heart, the real humans. The same type of thinking incited the brutality of the Christian-inspired Crusades and the Aryan white-supremacist led Holocaust.

By itself, name-calling conveys not facts, but instead encourages an emotional reaction that impairs good judgement. It is effective because it is simplistic, often comes across as humorous, and it is easy to remember like a slogan or label. However, like all propaganda, its intent is to short-circuit the reasoning process. The emotional reaction name-calling causes can shut down our thinking and suck us into accepting the opinion expressed by the name-caller. We owe it to ourselves to demand better, to demand clear and well-reasoned ideas, not immature name-calling. The last I was aware, they don't even allow such childish behavior on the playground at elementary schools. Why would we allow it in adult discourse?

A good example occurred in the 2016 election primaries when Donald Trump began calling his opponents names. Almost every opponent had a name or descriptive adjective that functioned like a name. Some names expressed crude sexual innuendos or cultural stereotypes. Little Marco garnered chuckles and at the same time undermined a comparison of the two candidates' policy positions. Does anyone remember what Marco Rubio had to say about tax policy, healthcare, or job creation?

Name-calling is a low-level trick that any person with freedom of thought can easily recognize as a below-the-belt punch, so to speak, and subversive. It makes an obvious attempt to steal our attention and logical thinking from the important issues. Demand that people respect your intelligence and don't allow them to stoop to this level of mud-slinging either by withholding any reaction to name-calling or by expressing your disdain for it.

VILIFICATION Propaganda

In recent decades vilifying other groups has become a fashionable method of solidifying support within one's own group. It is practiced on social media by trolls and increasingly in political debate. In so doing, sadly, we tear at the fabric that creates national unity and a country of which we are proud to be a part. What is worse, vilification too often results in avoiding discussing facts and the merits of positions on issues. Furthermore, we avoid looking for common ground that would allow us to find solutions. The result: no solutions and lots of animosity and disdain for each other. Not a healthy scenario for any country, community, or relationship. We are countrymen, and our quality of life will only improve if we learn to accept each other and build on this foundation of brotherhood.

It seems ironic that Americans have for centuries taken pride in the inscription at the base of our beautiful Statue of Liberty.

> "Give me your tired, your poor, your huddled masses yearning to breathe free, the wretched refuse of your teeming shore. Send these, the homeless, tempest-tossed to me, I lift my lamp beside the golden door!"   -- Emma Lazarus

Think about it. If America is a melting pot of various groups, but all those that we do not belong to are villainous, why would we want to live in America? Such a brainwash is unhealthy for national unity and weakens the group we call America. It is a vile and dangerous form of propaganda. It is the propaganda of the Nazis and fascists. The question to be asked is why we seem to tolerate this type of divisive propaganda, especially in social media and, increasingly, in our politics.

There was a time when vilification of others was dishonorable. Thus, this form of propaganda was less powerful. Recently, though, vilification has become an acceptable form of both political point-scoring and entertainment. Our acceptance of it leaves us vulnerable to the brainwashing effect it exerts on us. What is the answer to this problem for the free-thinker?

First, recognize it as false. It is not based on reason or logic. Second, avoid participating in the laughter and smiles shared when it is used. This is difficult, but to do otherwise encourages others to put logic aside for laughs and perhaps decisions. Standing up to the crowd is hard, but a simple "That's not cool" or "Not funny" or "Meanness does not make truth" and then changing the subject may work. I suggest you have a quick, easy response to use in these situations so that you can do your part in discouraging the proliferation of this form of propaganda and encourage reasoned approaches to both issues and people. Joking around and supporting vilification propaganda is a fine and difficult line that rarely and maybe never yields positive results.

FEAR MONGERING Propaganda

Fear is another not-so-subtle, but sinister, propaganda technique. It is probably the most used technique in politics and advertising. Because the emotion of fear is so very powerful, it is of utmost importance that free-thinkers recognize when fear is being generated during a discussion, speech, or advertisement. Fear, of course, can be created in many ways. Threatening words such as "He's going to start a war" or "You can lose your right to own a gun if so-and-so is elected" do not necessarily reflect facts, but if accepted without question will lead people to make decisions based on the fear of unsubstantiated claims.

There are at least three aspects to solving the problem of fear-induced mind control. First, recognize the fear and, second, seek the facts, knowing that the fear itself is not the same as the facts. And third, refuse to let the fear cause you to jump to conclusions or make assumptions. Franklin D. Roosevelt famously said, "The only thing we have to fear is fear itself." The message here is that fear will undermine our reasoning if we so allow. Therefore, when the powerful emotion is stirring inside, even if it is a very subtle stirring, we must double down on separating fact from fiction and using thought that is free of fear to examine the facts with clear thinking, and only then come to a logical decision or response. The challenge, of course, in today's information-saturated world is how to separate fact from fiction, the subject of chapter seven.

Another solution is to identify the generic fears you harbor inside. We all have certain fears, and when considering an issue, it is helpful to recognize preconceived ideas based on fear. Sometimes our fears stem from prejudices or stereotypes and may not be based on facts. For example, many people fear –isms: fascism, socialism, Islamism, Budhism, etc., etc. But do we really understand what the –ism we fear is? Make sure you have the facts so you can determine if the fear you feel is warranted. Some fears have validity, but other times our fear is of a world that is not what we have grown comfortable with, a fear of change. In this instance, we must look at potential change and ask ourselves if the harm outweighs the benefit of the change. We must also be careful to identify what the real harm is or whether the harm is only that my own world must adapt to the new and uncomfortable.

Several peer reviewed psychological studies have concluded that people who consider themselves conservative have a stronger reaction to fears than people who do not identify themselves as conservative.[7] However, no one is without fears, and in a changing world, our fears will change as well. Furthermore, no one is fully insulated from the propagandistic use of fear by others to try to motivate their behavior. Examine your own fears and whether each of your fears is worth being fearful about. Whether conservative or progressive, we all need to be self-aware and work to keep our brains free-thinking rather than fear-motivated.

BANDWAGON Propaganda

The name of this propaganda technique comes from a period in American history when an entertainer named Dan Rice campaigned for President Zachary Taylor with a band paraded down small-town streets on a wagon. As he marched through towns across the nation, he encouraged those in the crowd to "jump on the bandwagon" and support Taylor. After a successful campaign, the use of bandwagons in political campaigns became common place. However, the slogan "jump on the bandwagon" evolved to be quite derogatory. Today, this term describes people who thoughtlessly join the crowd or, worse, go against their own principles and beliefs just to be part of the majority or part of a winning group.

The technique, nowadays, is usually employed without the use of the slogan to avoid its derisive connotation. Nevertheless, joining the group has very strong emotional appeal as we learned in our analysis of Maslow's human needs hierarchy where it was noted that belonging is "probably one of the most powerful" needs humans have. Since this need is so powerful, it is easy to get sucked in by this propaganda even when we recognize its use. Recognizing the use of propaganda is not the same as not being influenced by it. Often our emotional need to belong and feel a part of a social group will play in the background of our thought processes.

Psychological research has shown that people often believe first, then look for evidence to support their "pre-conceived belief" (See explanation in chapter 5). If, as some think, the human brain evolved to react by sometimes adopting beliefs before seeking evidence as part of its survival mechanism, then we are faced with a very great challenge to our free-thinking efforts. Indeed, we must constantly evaluate the relationship between our beliefs and our reasoning to ensure that our beliefs are based on logic, not emotion or some psychological need lurking in our sub-conscience.

But, of course, we must first recognize the propaganda. There are many ways to say "Jump on the bandwagon" without using this phrase. One could use a very direct "Join us," or a subtler "Everybody's doing it." These types of statements are commonplace in advertising, and I suggest you practice looking for them and other propaganda techniques when watching television. The practice will help you become better attuned to propaganda in other areas of life as well.

The bandwagon technique is effective when we assume the opinion or practices of the majority (or group) is always valid. But an appeal to popularity (Latin: argumentum ad populum) only proves that a belief or practice is popular, not that it is true or better than alternative beliefs.

Many literary writers have incorporated this hasty conclusion fallacy into fictional novels in an attempt to warn us of its dangers. School teachers warn children of the dangers of caving to peer pressure. The bandwagon technique is a form of peer pressure exerted using subtle statements like "Ten million American can't be wrong, can they?"

This pressure tactic becomes more powerful and dangerous when it is combined with fear-mongering. In *The Crucible* by Arthur Miller, the character Abigail begins to name women she falsely claims she saw "dancing with the Devil." Betty joins in and soon several other girls "jump on the bandwagon" to name people they claim they saw with the Devil. The fear of this evil coupled with the pressure of the bandwagon fervor of the girls leads adults to put to death several innocent women convicted of being witches based solely on the many girls' testimony, which was prompted by peer pressure rather than truth. Mr. Miller's fiction is based on a real event in our Puritan history referred to as The Salem Witch Trials. The theme, as you can tell, is the danger of jumping on the bandwagon.

Majority opinion is simply not always valid. There was a time when everyone believed the world was flat, a time when many believed slavery was good and righteous, a time when most Americans supported going to war with Iraq believing it possessed weapons of mass destruction, which turned out to be untrue. It isn't always easy to get to the truth, especially when people in leadership positions deliberately deceive us, but a democracy demands this responsibility of its citizens. Individuals who pride themselves in being free thinkers cannot allow themselves to accept without evidence the spoon-fed ideas of others. Those that believe our democracy is worth keeping strong and free will not let popularity or peer pressure replace their ability to reason and make logical decisions based on real evidence and true facts. Keep an eye on politicians. Many are guilty of harnessing public opinion by combining fear and bandwagon propaganda with few, if any, good facts as evidence, or they use manufactured facts to deceive citizens. This is not true of all politicians, of course. Many do have integrity and strive for noble goals while working in a system that often rewards those who fight dirty and unfairly. Finally, the fluctuation of majority opinion implies that a logically valid conclusion cannot be based on the majority alone. It is healthy to be skeptical and do your homework.

PLAIN FOLK Propaganda

You would think this technique would easily be recognized as phony and glaringly false when used by people with power, position, or wealth. It is simple enough to say or imply, "Hey, I'm just like you," or "I want the same things we all want." This propaganda appeal attempts to gain acceptance into the group of "regular" folks. There is nothing wrong with trying to gain acceptance if it is sincere and honest. The problem, of course, is that it is often insincere and dishonest. Often, this propaganda is being used to hide true motives and intentions. Although it is found in advertising, politicians are the worst culprits.

It works like this. If they get you to believe they are like you, then you will accept them. If you accept them, then you may begin to trust them or like them.

Once you like a politician, research shows you are likely to vote for the apparently likable person without using your reasoning to evaluate the person's policies or agenda. Remember, also, that once you believe this candidate is the best choice, research shows you will look for reasons to support your belief and you will rationalize your decision. You will toss your free-thinking out the window and go into automatic support mode. In other words, you will see in this candidate only what you want to see.

The best solution: recognize when plain-folk propaganda is being used or incorporated into an argument. Recognize that if this propaganda is being incorporated into an argument, it is not a logical part of the argument, but only a tool to soften the mind of the audience and gain their acceptance and willingness to believe the argument— whether real facts back it up or not.

As a free-thinking citizen, your job is to find and examine the facts and determine if they are true and then to evaluate if the arguments are strong and sound compared to the counter-arguments.

TESTIMONIALS as Propaganda

Witness the number of people who make out like bandits by selling themselves as propaganda tools to advertisers. Every well-known sports hero and many celebrities cash in on their unique ability to provide testimonials. Some professionals, doctors and lawyers in particular, sell themselves for this use as well.

The testimonial propaganda form is very easy to recognize. Usually a famous person claims to have had great success using a product, and since he/she highly recommends it, you should rush out to purchase the product. Parents often suffer the consequences when their teens will accept only the sneaker recommended by one of their sports heroes. But let's face it, if a gorgeous or handsome actor recommends a product, adults may insist on at least trying it, especially if it promises to make us anywhere near as gorgeous or handsome as the person promoting the product. If we do what the rich, famous, and glamorous do, we are just a little bit closer to being one of them, right?

Another form of testimonial uses a professional who can tout their credentials to convince you to trust their paid-for-opinion. Doctors advertise drugs and other cures, professional weigh-lifters advertise weight lifting machines, chefs advertise kitchen gadgets, and the list goes on and on. By using their particular food chopper, grinder, or liquefier, you too can be an amazing chef, no doubt. That's all it takes. You get the picture.

Testimonials attempt to get us to associate a trait of the grand person claiming a product works with the ownership or use of the product. Wealth, physical attributes, etc. may be ours if we use the product for which a testimonial has been given.

Every politician tries to find a famous singer, band, actor, and sports hero to jump on the bandwagon and offer a testimonial and belief about how much the politician understands you and cares about you, and is a regular guy just like you. Then, of course, having a few professionals vouch for the politician's ideas is convincing as well. After all, the professionals must know what they are talking about, and they must be trustworthy, right? Economists, legal professionals, healthcare professionals, immigration enforcement officers will tell us why so-and-so's policy will work. And, of course, these professionals contradict one another right and left. Who are we to believe?

Honestly, there is no perfect substitute for doing your own research. It's that simple, but it is not so easy. The internet offers a wealth of help, but the trick is twofold. One, we have to be sure we are reading only credible sources, and two, we must avoid reading only information that supports the belief we already have or are leaning toward. (More on this in Chapters 5 and 6.) This takes self-discipline and the examination of conscience and self-awareness discussed earlier in this book.

Another problem is finding the time to figure out what professionals spend their careers figuring out. Here is where I turn to books and the library. Let's say I'd like to have a good understanding of how basic economics works. Finding a book on the subject by a reputable author allows me to teach myself about the subject in the quiet of my home where I can concentrate and weigh the evidence, arguments and explanations without the distraction of the propaganda found at political rallies and sometimes in media interviews and analysis. I can also read the ideas of other reputable professionals that disagree with the author I first read. I can take the time to search my own logical brain to decide which arguments and analysis seem to be the most correct.

It's a good idea to simply tune out people who are being paid to give their opinion or recommendation. Such testimonials are suspect. Instead, seek out, on your own, professionals that you believe do not have motives outside simply sharing their experience and expertise. Look to these people for guidance. Finally, be sure to listen to more than one person and to evaluate the counter-arguments or opposition side to make sure you reduce the possibility of incorporating your own or anyone's bias or pre-conceived ideas into your decisions.

TRANSFER or ASSOCIATION Propaganda

You've heard the phrase "guilt by association"? Transfer or association propaganda attempts to pin either the negative or positive emotions associated with a word, idea, person, or institution onto another person or institution in order to either put down or lift up the latter in the minds of the audience. Name-calling may be a form of transfer propaganda if the name used is strongly associated with specific traits. A clear example is the highly negative associations most Americans feel when someone is called a nazi, a fascist or an imperialist. WWI and WWII are seared into American culture thanks to the atrocities of Hitler and other fascist regimes. The American movie industry has done its part to keep us enlightened about why we went to war to fight these ideologies.

Transfer propaganda is difficult to notice when it is used with subjective terms like patriotism and loyalty, or with symbols such as the American flag or war veteran statues. But it is in this arena that transfer propaganda is most insidious, subversive, and dangerous. Let's use the four examples listed to illustrate how transfer propaganda works.

Most logical adults can acknowledge that patriotism can be expressed in many ways, and therefore, no one way of expressing patriotism determines whether a person is patriotic. Acknowledging this truth, we can agree that soldiers are not the only patriots. Many people who choose to work in lower paying jobs that serve our nation such as K-12 teachers and non-profit workers providing disaster relief and other services may deserve credit for patriotism as well as altruism. Unfortunately, some people and politicians will vilify a single stance on an issue as unpatriotic. Let's use taxes as an easy illustration.

If politician A believes tax cuts are needed to energize the economy and politician B believes tax cuts are irresponsible because it will put a burden on future generations by running up the national debt, one or the other may try transfer propaganda by calling the other politician unpatriotic because of his/her stance on this issue. Obviously, neither is unpatriotic; each simply believes in or promotes a different perspective. Each perspective probably has merits, but to call either unpatriotic is subversive. It attempts to subvert free-thinking and the expression of one's values with respect to taxes. It also attempts to manipulate those not strong in free-thinking to believe one perspective is unpatriotic and so anti-American. Such poor thinking skills combined with peer pressure and other propaganda led to the success of Nazi Germany and other dangerously illogical ideologies in both third world countries and some supposedly advanced countries. Unchecked, this type of propaganda is perilous for democracy.

Another less obvious example that is even more subversive and damaging to American democracy is the case in 2017 in which athletes exercising their Constitutional right to free speech chose to kneel during the national anthem in protest of police abuse of power. Risking retribution while lawfully standing up for what is a Constitutional right should be recognized by all as the epitome of patriotism. Some people felt that not standing for the national anthem was disrespectful and, therefore, unpatriotic. Using transfer propaganda and labeling the athletes and their act of protest as unpatriotic worked on people who could not think logically to recognize that taking a risk in order to stand up for Constitutional rights of others is true patriotism. Furthermore, as people and some in the media jumped on the bandwagon against the athletes, threats begin to be made and some even suggested violating the athletes' Constitutional rights in order to punish them. What nonsense! Yet, patriotic Americans fell for the propaganda put in front of them.

Standing for our national anthem may indeed show respect and patriotism, but it is not the only way to be a patriot, and it is likely that many simply stand out of habit. It's easy and it risks nothing. Kneeling demonstrated a reasoned and patriotic choice to deliberately shake things up and shed light on a wrong in our society that needed to be fixed. The willingness to take a principled stand and to accept its consequences took courage, as it most often does, and is obviously another way to show patriotism.

Still, the President himself, attempting to take advantage of the situation for his own gain, tried to use this transfer propaganda and declared the athletes unpatriotic while calling for their firing. This confused many who simply trusted the President's opinion rather than use their own free-thinking abilities and recognize the opportunistic use of transfer propaganda. A tragic result of having such a high-stature person as the President of the United States insert himself subversively into this issue was that several countries around the world jumped on the bandwagon and enacted laws to restrict free speech in the name of patriotism.

Similar confusion and controversy have been created around the treatment of our national flag. Narrow-minded people struggle to separate the flag from principles of freedom and democracy. Some think the treatment of the flag (stepping on it, burning it, etc.) as equal to denouncing our country and our values. Remember, it was not the flag our forefathers fought for, but the values expressed in our Declaration of Independence and later in our Constitution.

Free-thinking citizens can recognize that the symbol of the flag and what it symbolizes are two different things and agree with our Supreme Court that how the flag is treated is simply a form of free expression (speech), and by itself, is neither patriotic nor unpatriotic, right nor wrong— it is simply an act of expression protected by our First Amendment. Finally, logical thinking allows us to easily recognize that the treatment of statues falls into the same category.

In the heat of a passionate speech or eloquent rant, it is easy to forget to be skeptical and to neglect our responsibility to step back and analyze rather than allow ourselves to be persuaded by transfer propaganda that is powerful and compelling, even though illogical and ultimately nonsense. Beware the mistakes made in the fervor generated for the purpose of manipulation and captivation.

GLITTERING GENERALITIES

Similar to transfer propaganda, glittering generalities use the positive connotation of "virtue" words. Words such as *democracy, family*, and *patriotism* as well as value words such as *honor*, *loyalty,* and *duty*. It uses these "glittering" words to "adorn" a person or side of an issue. By associating the positive aspects with someone or some idea, people feel positive about that someone or idea.

Most politicians parade their families around to show they have "family values." They also make sure the cameras are rolling when they light candles in a church, shake hands with people in the military, hug a baby, etc. By themselves these acts tell us very little about the person (and many of them are planned purely for their effect). However, the positive association with "glittering" goodness helps an audience feel good about the person even though our response is purely emotional and not based in rational thought.

Contemporary Americans are often skeptical of what they see staged on television, knowing it has been deliberately set up by a marketing expert paid to take advantage of any glittering situations a person, politician, or movie star may find available to them. However, when glittering generalities are used in speeches and regular discourse, it can slip through the radar of our awareness. Similar to not judging a book by its fancy cover, we need to withhold judgement until we've had time to separate the show or showy words from the ideas, issues, or the person glowing in the stardust, so to speak. Most of us understand that what persons do for effect does not always represent what is in their hearts.

UNSUBSTANTIATED CLAIMS Propaganda

This insidious propaganda technique is basic lying for convenience. Some people will fake support for the prevarication by starting the lie with words like "Many people have said…" or "Many people believe…" or "I heard someone say…." If anyone dodges telling specifically where he or she got the information being put forth, be skeptical, don't fall for it. Demand proof— especially if that person is trolling for your dollars or your vote.

Unsubstantiated claims are often coupled with fear propaganda. It's quite common for people to claim that one candidate will take away your guns or that terrorists are streaming into our country, both invoking a lie and manipulating the powerful emotion of fear.

In our 2016 election cycle, this propaganda technique was used more ubiquitously than we have seen in recent history, and I believe it caught everyone off-guard. Instead of challenging the lies, our media let it go for quite a while, leaving citizens and other candidates to take on the challenge. Why would people in the media ignore an obvious lie? The answer resides in the tradition of reporting only what is said and letting others outside the media say otherwise. This was once considered appropriate of unbiased reporting when it was believed a reporter should not insert him or herself into the story. Now, however, this is seen as being complicit in promoting someone's false narrative. Of course, once the media was branded as fake news, their ability to challenge candidates' lies became weak and less consequential. (Note: Fake news exists, but reputable media outlets such as *The Wall Street Journal, The New York Times, The Washington Post* and others do not engage in deliberate fake news, and good media outlets will correct any errors in their reporting as soon as they realize an error has been made. It is our job to find and use media that has this level of integrity and to avoid giving our support to other media outlets. It is also our job to recognize the difference between reporting and opinion writing, knowing that the latter is not held to the same standards of factuality and truth as reporting. More on this in chapter 7.)

So, one can find many examples of the use of unsubstantiated claims, but the point is that a free-thinking citizen will never allow anyone to spoon feed them a crock of manure. Free thinkers will demand evidence and substantiation for all claims. Free thinkers will challenge the legitimacy of anyone's claims: journalists, T.V. commentators, politicians, and friends that assault their integrity by trying to lie to them or refusing to substantiate a claim. When someone tries to get away with lying, he or she takes their audience for fools, and if we allow for it or make excuses for lying, we are indeed fools.

What about exaggeration? If its not true, its not true. Exaggeration is not true. Some authors have discussed exaggeration as a separate propaganda technique, but in my mind, a lie is a lie. No need to dance around this fact. Call it what you want.

UNWARRANTED EXTRAPOLATION Propaganda

This form of propaganda draws a conclusion from facts that, although facts, are not bona fide evidence of the conclusion. The conclusion may or may not be true, but the facts provided prove nothing. Here's an example. *"The war has been going on for seven years. If we keep doing what we've been doing, the war will go on another seven years."* The factors involved in determining the length of a war are many, but its current duration is not one of them. Demand the relevant facts.

How about this? *"Illegal immigrants are breaking the law, so they are all dangerous criminals, and many are terrorists."* Whoa! Most immigrants, both legal and illegal, leave their home countries for a chance at a better life. This sentence provides no facts that support the conclusions. In addition, it plays on fear to intensify the effect of the propaganda. There is no reason given to believe that the group of people who immigrated illegally would have a greater percentage of dangerous criminals or terrorists than any other group of people. If you are against illegal immigration, no problem, but have the integrity to use relevant facts to argue your case and do not use unsubstantiated extrapolation. Free thinkers demand it.

This final example of unwarranted extrapolation is very popular but likely represents wishful thinking: *"Reducing corporate taxes will lead to higher wages because corporations will have more money."* Wouldn't it be nice, but show me the facts that back this up? Demand warranted substantiation. Historically, higher wages have not resulted from lower corporate taxes. In fact, they have led to increased stock holder profits, exorbitant CEO salaries and benefits, and huge income inequality. My research shows that some factors that have actually led to higher wages include unions and higher minimum wages. You do the research, free thinkers. Don't take my word for it.

SLOGANS as Propaganda

Some are catchy, some are duds, but slogans are definitely not rational arguments. Sometimes they are based on fears or glittering generalities or emotional desires, but they are never logical reasoning. As such, free thinkers will not be impressed by their crowd appeal and their emotional drumbeat. Slogans are simply part of marketing and propaganda campaigns. They are effective because they simplify the message, so the audience doesn't have to think, and they have come to be an expected part of political campaigns. Sad to say, some people really do want the audience not to think. It's not good for democracy, but it seems to be good at winning popularity and votes. It's also good at rousing crowd appeal and generating the energy that gets everybody on the bandwagon of support. It is, in short, an excellent propaganda technique, and no politician would be without one.

BAIT & SWITCH Propaganda

Bait and switch advertising is illegal because it is blatantly deceptive and false. An example from advertising is when something is offered, but when the consumer goes to collect, it is no longer available. However, a more expensive product is offered. In politics, something may be offered or promised with no intention of delivering. I believe the remedy here is to demand that politicians publish in writing the plans they have to back up their promises. If a politician does not do this, he/she is not likely to keep his/her promises. Governing in a democracy is tough in part because compromise is the only way to make long-term sustainable improvements. Without a plan to deal with competing interests and concerns, long-term solutions are not likely to be implemented. Look for a plan to back up promises.

DISTRACTING to AVOID an ISSUE

Although not propaganda per se, there are a few forms of distraction that are used frequently to avoid giving a straight answer. These distractions attempt to cloud an issue with irrelevant questions or concerns. Like propaganda, the technique avoids dealing with the relevant facts and seeks to convince the listener that the person speaking has a good answer to the problem. Free-thinking individuals need to be aware of these distractions.

WHAT-ABOUT-isms

If you are on your toes, you will notice when, instead of answering a question, a person says, "But what about…" and inserts something that, even though it may sound related, is only being brought up so the real issue can be dodged. Beware the deceptive question, "But what about…?" Hold the person's feet to the fire and demand an honest and legitimate answer to the question or concern. And work to notice when interviewers fail to challenge a what-about dodge. The best will not let this go unchallenged, but our responsibility is even more important in preserving our personal free thinking.

I KNOW YOU ARE Distraction

This childhood trick should get adults a little pissed off, but it does not seem to get under the skin of supporters. In fact, supporters ignore it as being a distraction and hail it as a legitimate concern. In this distracting technique the person will accuse someone else (usually an adversary) of the wrongdoing he himself is being accused of. In 2017 a few journalists picked up on the history of Donald Trump in using this technique. Observing the history analytically, I concluded that many times when Mr. Trump used this technique, he was accusing someone else of something he was himself guilty of having done. Whether his base supporters ever picked up on this is an interesting question.

EMOTIONAL TIRADES

Every parent has witnessed a child go into an emotional meltdown when he/she has been caught red-handed in a no-no. The child, of course, would like you to be distracted from his/her sin. Easy to notice—in fact, designed to get noticed— the emotional tirade can be used to distract, or it may be sincere. It is our job to determine which. I suggest asking yourself, "Is there something the person having an emotional tirade is avoiding?" Gotcha! This one is an insincere distraction. Call it out.

CONCLUSION

Propaganda works, in part, because the language of propaganda is colorful and it causes emotionally passionate reactions. Not only does it entertain us, it incites us. Our reactions to propaganda can be fierce. On the other hand, logic and reasoned deliberation, though capable of inspiring, are less likely to incite fierce emotions. Propaganda can create an emotional reaction that is addictive. The good news is that human intelligence can rise above the emotional high propaganda can create—if we are willing to think instead of simply react, and if we value reason more than passion and entertainment. Afterall, citizenship is not a reality television show. We're talking real consequences for our country and our democracy.

There are many tricks and traps used in marketing both commercially and politically, and there are many publications and university classes that examine them in much greater detail than done here. The citizen who desires to avoid being misled or duped must first learn to recognize the tricks of the trade. However, simply recognizing propaganda techniques is only the first step.

The second step is being self-aware. How are you reacting? If you are ignoring what you recognize, why? Are you making excuses for the perpetrator? Are you caught up in the emotional entertainment value of the manipulation and perhaps enjoying the controversy it may bring about? Are you letting yourself go along without challenging the corruption propaganda brings to our public discourse because you believe this demonstrates your loyalty to a cause? What about your loyalty to democracy and America?

Hitler is credited with coining the phrase "Your honor is your loyalty." He went on to convince the Nazi party members that to ever question a person in authority (Hitler's men) was disloyal and dishonorable. Free-thinking people know this corrupt idea distorts both honor and loyalty. If we know someone to be in error, and if that error poses a danger to others or to our country, it is our duty to correct it. That is the honorable course of action whether it is perceived as loyal or disloyal. That is patriotism. And we must note that the danger we are talking about is not just physical— it is also the danger posed when people are led to believe what is not true. It is the danger posed when those same people vote in an illegitimate leader based on false information. It is the danger that threatens a democracy when free-thinking individuals allow others to be blinded by the tricks and traps of propaganda.

Chapter 4

Herd Instinct

Are you part of the tribalism phenomenon?

Check your values at the door, thank you. You're either with us or against us. Your honor is your loyalty.

Really?

Is political party or religious affiliation more important than issues or even values in picking the leaders of our country? Has herd instinct overtaken our logical thinking and analysis when it comes to voting? Are the pep rallies, pep talks, and propaganda of politicians more important to our decision-making than our free-thinking? Are you using easy, one-sided or even careless methods of determining which candidate you support and your position on issues?

Our democracy demands self-examination in response to the troublesome developments of our politics. What has caused us, in recent years, to become so vehemently and blindly loyal to the groups we associate with? And since it is so often *blind* loyalty, how can we break free of it so we can use our logical and free-thinking ability to determine our positions on important issues and determine where we can compromise and work together to forge solutions. After all, we can probably agree that a free-thinking mindset would be better for our country in terms of both national unity and national strength. The "It's our way or no way" attitudes of the extreme right and left only result in grinding government to a halt. With such attitudes, democracy cannot survive. It may be slow, but the heart of democracy is compromise. We gotta get along, guys.

Jonathan Haidt explores the research on the problem of tribalism in his book *The Righteous Mind, Why Good People are Divided by Politics and Religion,* and I highly recommend a thorough reading to best understand this phenomenon. Haidt examines how morality evolved in humans and how our rational minds interact with our intuitive beliefs. His research, he argues, shows that Americans are driven politically by the emphasis they place on a set of five basic values: caring, fairness, loyalty, authority, and sanctity.[8]

Many people seem to believe that members of the opposition political party either have no values, or their values are not the same values shared by those in their political party. The reality, according to Haidt, is that we simply emphasize different values and interpret some values in different ways. For example, the fairness value is important to people in both parties. However, one party sees fairness as helping those who have had fewer opportunities in life to get ahead. The other party sees fairness as allowing people to enjoy the fruits of their hard work without expectation of sharing those fruits with others, who they perceive as not having earned them. Their religion may ask them to be generous with their blessings, but their government should not. Both positions are logical, and both are based on the value of fairness seen from different perspectives. This idea, that the way we emphasize our values determines our politics, is contrary to the long-standing assumption that we gravitate toward our parents' political party affiliation.

Haidt explains that once we begin to develop our political identities and philosophies, we search for and gather up the reasons and evidence that support our beliefs and filter out the truths that challenge or contradict our beliefs. This natural tendency is a result of our evolution where intuition served as the faster tool in avoiding danger. Our brains once needed (and so evolved) to evaluate instantly and constantly. Hence, intuitive belief comes naturally before rational thought and evaluation. We feel something is right and it seems logical, so we look for the evidence and logic that will support our belief and ignore or even deny contradictions, even when those contradictions are true.[9]

In his book *The Believing Brain*, Michael Shermer backs up Mr. Haidt's conclusions related to the human tendency to rely on intuition to the detriment of our reasoning. He writes,

> "For now, keep in mind that research consistently shows that once people have established what they think is the cause of an event they just observed— (in other words, they have formed a link between A and B)— they will then continue to gather information to support that causal link over other possibilities— if they can even think of alternatives once their first causal link is established, which they usually cannot" (p.82).[10]

The free-thinking person (to truly be free) must be willing to challenge his/her own beliefs and the beliefs of his/her herd(s)—the group(s) he/she feels an affinity toward—to play devil's advocate, if you will, and to be open-minded about considering all sides and truths regarding a problem or issue.

To this end, we must take time to "walk in other people's moccasins" so to speak. Stereotyping others is itself unfair and illogical. We must seek out the facts to bring logical thinking to an issue—while avoiding "group think" or herd mentality (another word for tribalism).

Yes, there was a time in our long ago human history when staying close to the herd or tribe was smart for survival, but our brain development will now allow us to invoke logic rather than blind fear or loyalty—if we are willing to learn how. It is neither natural nor automatic. It must be deliberately practiced with critical self-examination in the privacy of one's own heart and mind.

Sure, we still have a strong emotional need for group acceptance as discussed in Maslow's Hierarchy of Needs, but we also have the intelligence to analyze when our group is right or wrong, fair or prejudiced, etc. And, hopefully, we have the integrity, patriotism, and courage to be within a group and still stand for what is true, logical, and right.

I'm not saying it is easy, but allowing the people we care about to operate with ideas that have been brainwashed into them is perhaps a form of disloyalty to both our loved ones and our country, and to any herd to which we choose to belong.

Another cause of herd instinct or tribalism is what David Brooks identified as "The Siege Mentality Problem" in his opinion piece published in *The New York Times*, 11-13-17. Brooks asserts,

> "In fact, I'd say the siege mentality explains most of the dysfunctional group behavior these days, on left and right. You see the siege mentality not just among evangelical Christians, but also among campus social justice warriors, and gun lobbyists, in North Korea and Iran, and in the populist movements across Europe."[11]

Brooks explains that this mental frame of mind is developed when a group feels what he calls "collective victimhood." It's not just about having adversaries, but the group begins to feel the "whole culture or the whole world is irredeemably hostile" to their group. From this siege mentality overwhelming fear takes hold as people in the group increasingly come to believe that "the world our children inherit will be horrific."[12]

The siege mentality gives people a sense of being part of a group that although underdogs will stick together for their noble cause and fight the powerful ones that would destroy them or their culture. Brooks further argues,

> "The siege mentality also excuses the [group] leader's
> bad behavior. When our very existence is on the line, we
> can't be worrying about things like humility, sexual
> morality, honesty, and basic decency. In times of war all
> is permissible…. In the end, though, the siege mentality
> ends up being self-destructive."[13]

Brooks continues with the example of the Evangelicals in the 2016 election. Evangelical Christians, he says, "…had a humane model for leadership— servant leadership—but, feeling besieged, they swapped it for Donald Trump, for gladiator pagan leadership."[14]

Mmm...maybe yes, maybe no, but it is clear that being part of a religious group, just as being part of any group, could promote herd instinct or tribalism. So, it should be equally clear that we must guard against this fault. Letting others think for you or accepting what others promote as righteous and true without engaging your own logical thinking is dangerously absurd. We are all human and prone to human mistakes. Each of us has our own brain. Perhaps that was by design and for a logical reason.

Conclusion

It makes sense to me that siege mentality as well as other forms of tribalism would become self-destructive. When you take free and logical thinking out of people's decisions, those people will eventually be rejected by others who have not ceded their brain power to fear and herd instinct.

So, do not check your values at the door, thank you, or your logic and ability to think for yourself. As Maslow asserts, you may have an emotional need to belong to the group; and as Haidt's research shows, you may try to ignore the facts that contradict your beliefs; or as Shermer explains, you may struggle even to see alternatives to what you believe; and there may be times, Brooks asserts, when you feel the whole world is out to destroy what you deeply believe in. Still, turn to your ability to think. And insist your thinking be free of the brainwashing forces of herd instinct, or propaganda, or other forces that would have you follow blindly. In doing so, you may also be able to lead others out of this darkness and away from being brainwashed.

Chapter 5

Confirmation Bias
A Demon Lurking Within?

In addition to Maslow's Needs Hierarchy and Herd Instinct, we also have to contend with the internal influence of our own confirmation bias, which may be the most ubiquitous threat to our freedom of thought. Just as the cowboy lost in the desert may think he sees the ripple of water and an oasis of lush green trees, so too our desire to see what we need or want to see may lead us to believing in an information mirage, supposed facts and logic that are not actually there. Although confirmation bias has been referred to in previous chapters, it requires a full explanation and understanding.

What is Confirmation Bias

Confirmation bias is a prejudice within human psychology to find evidence and facts for what we already believe and to ignore or discount evidence and facts against the beliefs we already have. Confirmation bias is difficult to overcome, especially if those in the groups we associate with give us positive support for our bias. Often people assume it is the uneducated that are most susceptible to this phenomenon within the brain, but the opposite is true. People with high degrees of confidence are most inclined to this bias. High levels of education tend to lead to high levels of confidence. High levels of confidence support stubborn adherence to one's beliefs. Therefore, it is the more educated among us that are most vulnerable to becoming victims of their own confirmation bias. Is it pride, over-confidence, or a glitch in our make-up that leads to confirmation bias? Perhaps someday we will fully understand, but for now, we will simply have to overcome it to protect our free thinking.

Why Confirmation Bias Undermines Free Thinking

Correcting confirmation bias is no easy task. People who believe in free will, a pillar of most religions, have the most difficult time recognizing and correcting this type of bias. I would argue this is so for at least two reasons. First, we want to feel confident in our beliefs, so we have little inherent motivation to recognize confirmation bias at work within ourselves. The good news for Christians is that the Bible in the words of Jesus directs us *"Thou hypocrite, cast out first the beam out of thine own eye; and then shalt thou see clearly to cast out the mote of thy brother's eye."* Thus, we have been warned by Jesus that we may harbor biases we do not recognize within ourselves. Second, doubting ourselves is uncomfortable, and for some may, I believe, lead to decision paralysis. In other words, once we entertain doubt, making a choice is risky. Instead of kicking our rational analysis ability into gear and determining what is actually true or well-reasoned, we disengage and either make no choice or revert to our bias.

Furthermore, confirmation bias is multi-faceted. There are so many types of confirmation bias that it stands to reason that none of us will likely overcome it at every opportunity. Still, we must give it our best shot because our democracy will be stronger if our citizens, all of us, are clear thinking.

This chapter explains those types of confirmation bias that are most threatening to free-thinking citizens whose goal is to support wise decisions for their country. For a more thorough understanding of the various types of confirmation bias in easy-to-understand laymen's language, I highly recommend Michael Shermer's book *The Believing Brain, Chapter 12.* Indeed, this is a must read for those interested in the psychology of belief in general. According to Shermer, we actually have an idea of where in the brain the confirmation bias is processed because of an fMRI study by Drew Weston conducted at Emory

University. How cool is that! It is a first step toward understanding this unfortunate mechanism built into our human psyche.

Sunk Cost Bias

Upton Sinclair said, "It is difficult to get a man to understand something when his job depends on not understanding it." When we have invested our effort, emotions, time, money, etc. in something we believe in, it is extremely difficult to come to the realization that our investment has been misguided and perhaps wasted on an incorrect belief or conviction; so, we hold on steadfastly even when the ship is sinking. We are often not rational about it. We all know of people (maybe ourselves) who have not acted rationally in finance, in love, in politics, and more. War is a tragic illustration of American leaders' sunk cost bias. Since WWII, at least two American wars have continued for over a decade in the futile attempt to show families and friends back home that the loss of their loved ones was not in vain or to save face for our countrymen. For those of us who remember it, the Vietnam War still haunts us for the realizations of our sunk cost bias that sacrificed so many young men both abroad and at home.

No one wants to jump ship, but the more rational approach is to assess costs versus the likelihood of a worthwhile benefit, then decide if it is time to cut your losses and abandon the false belief(s). This is the approach of the free-thinking citizen, the rational patriot.

Attribution Bias

If we are ever to overcome the polarities and divisiveness in our politics, we must understand and route out this bias. Although there are various types of this bias, it boils down to our tendency to attribute positive reasons for our beliefs and what we stand for, but negative reasons for the beliefs and goals of those not a part of our group. For example, people will try to back up a bias with an intellectual argument to show it is not a bias but rather a reasoned approach. On the other hand, people will treat others as if their perspectives are based solely on an emotional approach or some other less than well-reasoned slant. Obviously, this bias reinforces tribalism and herd instinct. It should be clear that the only way to find common ground and solve differences that may come from our bias is to acknowledge the reasoned approach of each side as well as all the emotions on both sides. It is usually also helpful to acknowledge one another's good intentions. This will start us on a path to solving differences and living together in peace and with compassion.

Status Quo Bias

Do you sometimes hold tight to what you know, to what has always been? Do you sometimes firmly refuse to consider changes or new methods for no other reason than "It's always been this way," or "We've always done it this way"? This is status quo bias, and it is probably the easiest form of confirmation bias to recognize in ourselves. In fact, this bias has been immortalized in the saying, "You can't teach an old dog new tricks." Some of us are proud of being "old dogs" while others of us fight the narrow-mindedness this implies. Because we can feel emotional stress when we are asked to make changes, we can recognize when status quo bias may be at work within us. Most of us, however, will admit we don't always fight it when we see this bias wielding its ugly head within our own psyche. Somehow it doesn't feel ugly. It feels like we are "being true to ourselves." Some of us even wonder, "If I give in, am I being a pushover?" Don't let these emotions cloud your free thinking. Step back and analyze.

Loss aversion is a symptom of status quo bias. We are more motivated to protect and keep what we already have and avoid risking loss than to pursue a gain.

Have you ever felt paralyzed to take the steps needed to start a new workout program even after you made a New Year resolution? Have you ever felt paralyzed to find a new job despite how miserable you feel in the current job? How many of us put off refinancing a home even when we know it could save us thousands of buckos? The fear of loss, making a mistake, losing some free time, etc. stops us from pursuing the positive benefits.

In our efforts to hone our free-thinking skills, we must commit to challenging this bias by considering with open minds the positive aspects of whatever change or new idea is presented. I like to use a cost/benefit analysis for each option set up in a simple T-chart. I list all the pros and cons of the options and then compare the charts. In comparing, I usually rate each positive and negative from most to least or from extreme to inconsequential. From here my choice is informed and more likely free of bias. For those of you using e-readers, I give you this URL to find a simple example of a T-chart (https://www.worksheetworks.com/miscellanea/graphic-organizers/tchart.html).

I recently did this when, after having put off surgery for two years, I was facing increasing difficulty working in my garden and training my dogs. What took me two years? In part, I knew what I had was tolerable, if not great, and I didn't know with certainty what I would get from surgery. The evidence was good for a good outcome. I researched the neurosurgeon and the hospital and talked to people who had recently had back surgery. Still, there were no guarantees. Next, I examined my own circumstances and the pros and cons of putting off a surgery that I knew was likely in my future despite my efforts at physical therapy and self-help. I weighed the counsel of the doctors and physical therapists I had worked with and my own convictions regarding my health. The surgery went quite well. I am now methodically working on my recovery and looking forward to my gardening and dog training as well as the backcountry llama packing we have not been able to do in three years. What took me so long? Status quo bias.

Framing Effect Bias

The way beliefs or facts are presented or framed can also lead to bias. We will tend to support the side presented that, in our minds, is framed most positively. It's worth noting that whenever we listen to or read a news article, we should be aware that the author is framing the story for us. That framing may be positive or negative to us. Since it is virtually impossible to tell a story without framing it in some way or other, it is our job to determine if our reaction toward our perception of it being positive or negative is biased. In order to determine this, we must examine the story framed differently. We must be willing to ask ourselves, "What is another way to think about this event?"

Here is an example.

> Negative Frame: Ten soldiers were killed today in a dangerous assault on an ISIS target outside of Fallujah, Iraq. Several enemy fighters were also killed in a war that has far exceeded the time frame announced last year by the President, who offered condolences to the grieving families and expressed confidence in our troops. He continues to assure the American public that our war efforts are not wasted and that no threat of terrorism will go unanswered here at home, claiming our presence in Iraq is insurance against attacks at home.

> More Positive Frame: Ten soldiers made the ultimate sacrifice in a daring assault while successfully killing several ISIS terrorists outside of Fallujah, Iraq. The President praised the men and expressed his gratitude for their patriotism to their proud families. Although the time frame announced for this war last year has been extended, the President continues to express confidence

our soldiers will soon be able to come home and that our country is far safer from terrorism because of our presence in Iraq.

Notice the more positive framing used in the second paragraph above. Both paragraphs tell the same story, but the first chooses words that frame the event negatively. *Dangerous assault* sounds unnecessary whereas *daring assault* sounds brave. *"Proud families"* sends the message that we, too, should be proud rather than *grieving* with the families of the first paragraph. The *far exceeded* time frame of the first paragraph makes it sound as though a promise has been broken. The words "our war efforts are not wasted" gives far less confidence than "our country is far safer." Which paragraph would lead you to be skeptical and which would lead you to support the continued fighting and "sacrifice"?

Of course, your answer would depend on the ideas you harbored before reading either of these paragraphs, but the framing of each could support the development of a bias about the war effort. Being aware that the story can be told from different frames of reference allows you to avoid being pushed into one bias or the other, positive or negative. And this allows us to do the analysis and, ideally, clear-minded examination of the facts to make a free-thinking judgment.

Anchoring Bias

This prejudice stems from not having the knowledge we need to effectively evaluate a belief or a decision. We don't know what we don't know. So, when we need to make a choice or evaluate, we will have a bias toward relying on what we already know (the easy path). Rather than taking the time to educate ourselves and learn about the issue, we may rush to judgement. In essence, we anchor ourselves to one piece of information or narrowly to what we already know. In so doing, we may be called "narrow-minded," and indeed, we are if we let this bias rule the day.

To avoid this bias, I recommend cultivating your curiosity. Pay attention to all the information around you, and when you must make a choice, avoid a rush to judgment by taking the time to seek out and read as much as you can on the issue. As always, read up on both sides, be open-minded, but check and verify the facts.

Availability Bias

The tendency to see in the numbers only evidence of what we already believe is a common trap that undermines our free-thinking. It is a compelling trap because "numbers don't lie," right?

When I first moved to Idaho twelve years ago, there was great controversy over the proliferation of wolves after their re-introduction to Idaho. Many local hunters in my neck of the woods claimed the wolves were killing too many elk. Their evidence was the fact that they weren't seeing as many elk during their hunts—and the numbers, of course, don't lie. The Fish and Game Department, however, confirmed that most of the elk herds in Idaho were healthy and growing. Still, local hunters believed the wolves were killing them off in big numbers just because the hunters didn't find as many available in the locations they once had found them. Perhaps the wolves were causing the elk to change their habits, but wolves were not decimating the herds as local hunters fervently believed. Idaho continues to have healthy elk herds despite wolf and human predation.

The availability bias requires us to be willing to consider other possible reasons or causes for what we see and even what we can count. In the same vein, we should look at statistics with some degree of skepticism. Remember, all statistics have a +/- error rating, which means it is accepted that the percentage could be wrong up or down by the amount of the rating. Furthermore, in the realm of statistics, numbers can be manipulated, hidden, and manufactured. Make sure you trust your sources and look for other sources that agree or corroborate what has been reported.

It's important to remember that much of the time we may not see the whole picture unless we are willing to look for it. This requires taking the time and doing the work (usually reading) needed to fully know the facts. This bias, as with others, can interfere with our free-thinking.

Self-justification Bias

When we make a decision and then go out to find the evidence that supports it, we are engaging in self-justification. This type of decision-making is biased; we really don't know if ours is the best possible decision since we have not taken the time to evaluate before we made it. Instead, we go looking for evidence after the decision is made. In so doing, we will avoid evidence to the contrary because we have invested our pride in a decision already made.

In my mind, self-justification bias is willful narrow-mindedness or willful prejudice. Sounds like something that should be outlawed, but in some ways it's a good thing that we are free to be ignorant if we so choose. However, I maintain it is a threat to our democracy, our way of life, our culture and our country. It takes great discipline to rid ourselves of bias, and the only way to do it is to actively question our initial reactions and thoughts, and to seek out all sides and all evidence and facts before our final decisions. This extra time and effort, however, pays off big dividends.

Blind Spot Bias

Finally, it is critical to recognize the bias blind spot. We all have a tendency to be able to see other people's biases yet not recognize our own. According to Guy P. Harrison, author of *Think* and *Think Before You Like,*

"…bias is a natural and standard process of the human subconscious mind. It's always on, working to keep us feeling smart and rational, even as it builds unrealistic, sometimes bizarre fantasy worlds inside our heads. We all have this bias but few of us realize just how relentless and influential it can be in its mission to support or confirm our observations, conclusions, and beliefs. It is the reason we so often see someone blatantly ignore or sidestep powerful evidence and logic when these things conflict with the person's previously held belief…. This is a cognitive process that people—you and me included—don't naturally recognize when it's happening. We believe ourselves to be consistently honest when it comes to assessing the world around us. But we fail at it every day of our lives in large part due to confirmation bias." (p.81)[15]

This is hugely problematic in a democracy for at least two reasons. First, it leads to pointing the blame finger at others while treating ourselves and our group as better, the "holier than thou syndrome." This, of course, leads to animosity, divisiveness, and such bad feelings that we become stubborn about listening and considering alternatives to our own beliefs. We close our minds and hearts to others. This is a real shame when we consider the wise saying, "Two heads are better than one."

A second problem the bias blind spot presents should be obvious. If we can't see our own bias, we certainly cannot correct it, and so we cannot truly be free-thinkers. Worse, we cannot be sure our decisions and choices are well thought out and, therefore, the best possible. This certainly isn't where any of us want to be.

Be aware of the bias blind spot, and accept that you will need to regularly make an examination of your own conscience to catch your own bias in order to reign it in. Frequently ask and honestly answer the question, "Do I have all the facts and evidence, and have I examined it with an open mind and an open heart, without prejudgment?" It takes discipline to be a free-thinker.

The Common-Sense Trap

So, in recognizing the types of confirmation bias (and I remind you my list is not exhaustive) we can understand that our intuition may not be, indeed likely is not, always reliable. In fact, knowing about confirmation bias should encourage us to avoid snap judgements and to investigate more carefully the hidden facts we may have missed.

The common-sense trap exists because we really don't know what we don't know. Because of this, what appears to be "common sense," based on what we do know may not be so sensible after we learn more about what we don't know. And because we all have varying degrees of knowledge and awareness, what is "common-sense" to one person may not be "common-sense" to another.

What Michael Shermer describes as the Middle Land aspect of the human brain and sensory capacity helps to explain why the common-sense trap exists. He explains that humans exist in what evolutionary biologist Richard Dawkins calls *Middle World*—a land midway between short and long, small and large, slow and fast, young and old.

> "In the middle land of space, our senses evolved for perceiving objects of middling size—between, say, grains of sand and mountain ranges. We are not equipped to perceive atoms and germs, on one end of the scale, or galaxies and expanding universes, on the other end. In the Middle Land of speed, we can detect objects moving at a walking or running pace, but the glacially slow movement of continents (and glaciers) and the bogglingly fast speed of light are literally imperceptible. Our Middle Land time scales range from the

> psychological "now" of three seconds in duration to the few decades of a human lifetime, far too short to witness evolution, continental drift, or long-term environmental changes. Our Middle Land folk numeracy leads us to pay attention to and remember short-term trends, meaningful coincidences, and personal anecdotes (p.277).[10]

We must question what is often called "common-sense" and exercise freedom of thought to determine if it is truly sensible. In fairness, we must acknowledge that we may not know all there is to know and search out that knowledge. Does that mean we should be paralyzed to act out of fear we have incomplete knowledge? No, but it does mean we should listen to others, be curious, read about those things we most care about, and always be open to new possibilities. It is our fate that we must make some decisions without full knowledge of every possible aspect of an issue or problem, but in this day and age, we have access to resources of which our parents could only have dreamed. So, when we have time, we have no excuse to be ill-informed. And in a democracy, we have a duty. So be it.

What About Science

Many people have come to distrust science as having its own bias. To be honest, we have learned that, despite the scientific method and rigorous peer review, sometimes scientific studies are faulty. Our bias is far-reaching, and the same cognitive temptations exist in scientists. After all, they are human beings just like the rest of us. It is important to recognize the extent to which the field of science has gone to purge bias from research studies. Double-blind controls are required of all experiments accepted as note-worthy. This means neither the subjects nor the experimenters know the conditions during data collection. Other scientists will judge the results by reviewing the methods and techniques employed and writing reviews of the findings. Best practices are expected to be taken seriously as good scientific research.   Furthermore, research results are never accepted as definitive until they have been repeated by other researchers in labs unaffiliated with the original scientist, and one replication is often not enough. Skepticism and questioning is encouraged. All reports must include any evidence that contradicts the findings as well as alternative interpretations of the data.

Still, as citizens, it is healthy to demand the highest level of rigor in scientific research and to expect that several studies corroborate one another before making conclusions. We must, unfortunately, be aware that some people will say anything if they are paid enough. I do not recommend getting your science from the news media. I recommend using the local librarian to help you find real science-based information on those issues of concern to you. Librarians are trained in finding true information and have access to many data bases and tools and techniques used to find reliable publications. They will usually tell you if you need to go to a bigger library or perhaps a specialty library. They should also be able to direct you to the library that would better serve your particular interest and need.

Shortcuts are hard to find when looking for reliable information. I have found it helpful to keep track of experts I believe I can trust so I can rely on their views and save the library trips for only the issues of the most critical importance to me. It takes discipline to be a free-thinker, but freedom of thought is the greatest freedom we have. In America and other democracies, people have the opportunity to achieve free thinking if we choose.

Chapter 6

Social Media & Active Measures

A Hotbed of Confirmation Bias and Echo Chamber Propaganda

My husband and I both taught computer-use to middle and high school students during our careers as teachers. Hubby enjoyed teaching high school students how to harness computer technology for artistic endeavors. I taught middle school kids research strategies and security issues on the internet. We have had many late-night discussions over whether the internet is a good thing or a bad thing for society and for our children. We both see the amazing opportunities for learning and information sharing, but having to teach personal security on the internet has exposed me to the many abuses people have found for this basically free tool. Responsibility is not a guaranteed feature of internet use. Social media platforms have fallen victim to human avarice, and social media users have become victims of that greed as well.

Filter Bubbles & Echo Chambers— How Social Media Isolates You

Every move on social media and much of the internet is tracked. Sophisticated algorithms, computer programs, turn your clicks into marketable information. Many of these computer codes take your input information and use machine learning (computer code that rewrites itself in response to your input) to produce responses to you. This allows ads to pop up about things in which you've expressed an interest. This system also allows news, both real and fake, to be fed to you based on the interests and beliefs you have input into your social media account. In so doing, it filters in the news for which you are most likely to have a confirmation bias and filters out the information with which you are likely to be uncomfortable, disagree with, or refuse to consider as possible.

This computer response to your input is commonly referred to as your filter bubble. It is also called the echo chamber because what you like gets sent to you repeatedly in slightly different form. This repetition acts just like a propaganda tool reinforcing and cementing your beliefs like stone—a stone that will take a sledge hammer to break up, whether it is true or false. That's just human nature.

Social media sites have been designed to send you information you want (like) and to filter out information you don't want (dislike). As we've learned, confirmation bias together with some basic psychology (Maslow's Hierarchy) will likely lead us to ignore or filter out those ideas or facts that contradict what we want to believe or what we already believe. When you add repetition to this phenomenon, you can see the tidal wave working against your free thinking. Social media is a tsunami of propaganda and confirmation bias. I believe social media is the greatest threat to democracy and free thinking the world has seen since Adolph Hitler. It is capable of destroying free thinking altogether if we do not recognize its power. Don't let it.

Does this commentary sound over-the-top? Of course, social media has and will have some positive effects. Crowd-funding and support for good causes is just one. However, the negative impacts of social media on democracy and civil discourse must be acknowledged and understood. During the February 25th 2018 episode of *Reliable Sources*, Glen Beck, a popular conservative political commentator and founder of *The Blaze*, said that the evidence shows that divisiveness in America has become increasingly widespread since the inception of Facebook. "Facebook and Twitter have added to this problem a great deal. If you look at where the average Democrat was and the average Republican was, if you look at the charts [they overlapped in their ideas and beliefs] until about 2006—the first year of Facebook, and we started moving apart. We are now vastly two different countries."[16]   For the record, Facebook launched in 2004, YouTube in 2005, and Twitter in 2006. Mr. Beck's point, however, is not lost. Social media has served more to divide us into ideological groups (or tribes) rather than to bring us together to understand one another—a direct result of the filter bubble phenomenon.

Making Money Off Your Likes

Facebook and other social media companies sell the capability of targeting users to paying customers (commercial companies, political groups, candidates, foreign countries, troll farms, etc.). The paying customers believe they can benefit from your attention. The companies providing access to you and your information do so almost exclusively to make money. They are, as of this writing, apparently not too worried about the propaganda and other persuasive techniques attempting (with frequent success) to interfere with your ability to think freely. Your well-being and the well-being of democracy is not their top priority—if they are concerned about it at all. Only very recently have some of these companies begun to be aware of the adverse impact their money-making algorithms can have and are having on democracy. And to date, what they are doing about it barely scratches the surface of the problem. We are on our own to protect our free thinking from the onslaught. The social media companies' allegiances are to those who pay, not to the users who play on their platforms.

Because of this money-making business model, the news and information we get on social media is more likely to have a biased agenda behind it versus traditional news sources. (Traits of traditional media sources are covered in the next chapter.) It should be obvious what a tremendous problem this presents to citizens dedicated to free and clear thinking. Social media participation, as of this writing, insures you will be constantly exposed to confirmation bias and propaganda, often working in tandem, to please and manipulate you with feel-good information for which you may have expressed a liking. It was designed this way.

I guess Mark Zuckerberg and other techno-wizards never read George Orwell's *1984* or Ray Bradbury's *Fahrenheit 451* (Recommended reading for all free-thinkers.) because, if they had, they might have realized what their algorithms and machine learning could do to our society. In fairness, Facebook, YouTube, Microsoft, Twitter, and later, Google and Snap, Inc. launched the Global Internet Forum to Counter Terrorism (GIFCT) in 2017. This laudable effort has the mission of disrupting terrorists' ability to use the internet and social media to further their causes. These companies are making other efforts, as well, but some of these companies have claimed that they are not media companies and so do not have the responsibility to prevent fake and misleading news from spreading on their platforms. My question: If not them, who? Until changes are made, the answer is us. In a free democracy, we all have the responsibility to prevent fake and misleading news from spreading in all venues of our society.

According to Guy P. Harrison, author of *Think Before You Like*,

> "Some concerns are external, such as the way social media companies collect and profit off users 'private data.'" He also states, "They also manipulate people's minds, hook them in ways not so different from how casinos manage to keep gambling addicts planted in front of slot machines for hours. Other concerns are internal…cognitive biases, mental shortcuts, perception problems, and emotional weak spots that can and do trip [people] up online….there is an urgent need for all users to arm themselves with knowledge about how social media companies operate, how our brains function online, and what steps we can take to protect ourselves (p.11)."[17]

Bots, sockpuppets, cyborgs, etcetera will be explained later in this chapter, but first we must look at the big picture of computational propaganda and learn about how our minds work in the online environment.

Computational Propaganda

It did not take very long for social media tech people to market their skills in developing software algorithms that could be used to manipulate how citizens think. These are powerful tools. If you control the most powerful tools, you are the most powerful, and power is indeed a most corrupting force. Computational propaganda is a term coined by researchers at the Oxford Internet Research Institute at the University of Oxford to describe the phenomenon of using algorithms, automation, and human coordination to purposefully distribute misleading information over social media networks to influence people's thinking. "Computational propaganda involves learning from and manipulating real people so as to manipulate public opinion…"[18] This section presents some of the findings of the University's research noted in the Executive Summary of Working Paper Number 2017.11, which addresses computational propaganda worldwide. Twelve researchers, across nine countries, interviewed 65 experts, analyzed tens of millions of posts on seven different social media platforms during scores of elections, political crises, and national security incidents between 2015 and 2017. The picture their findings present is of a clear and ominous danger to democracy and free thinking.

The working paper states that social media are significant platforms for political engagement and crucial channels for distributing news content. They are the primary media over which young people develop their political identities. In several democracies the majority of voters use social media to share political news and information, especially during elections. In authoritarian countries, social media platforms are a primary means of social control. This is especially true during political and security crises. In democracies, social media are actively used for computational propaganda either through broad efforts at opinion manipulation or targeted experiments on particular segments of the public. In each of the nine countries studied, including the United States, civil society groups struggled to protect themselves and respond to active misinformation campaigns, but their results were mixed. Russian use of automated accounts in the United States can be traced from fringe social networks with few followers to more mainstream core groups with significant numbers of followers.[18]

Interviews with political party operatives, freelance campaigners and elections officials in seven countries provide evidence that social media bots— and computational propaganda more broadly—have been used to manipulate online discussion. Some social media platforms, in particular political contexts, are either fully controlled by or dominated by governments and organized disinformation campaigns. Authoritarian governments direct computational propaganda at their own population and at populations in other countries. In democracies, individual users design and operate fake and highly automated social media. Political candidates, campaigns, and lobbyists rent larger networks of accounts for purpose-built campaigns while governments assign public resources to the creation, experimentation and use of such accounts.[18]

> Regimes use political bots, built to look and act like real citizens, in efforts to silence opponents and to push official state messaging. Political campaigns, and their supporters, deploy political bots—and computational propaganda more broadly—during elections in attempts to sway the vote or defame critics. Anonymous political actors harness key elements of computational propaganda such as false news reports, coordinated disinformation campaigns, and troll mobs to attack human rights

defenders, civil society groups, and journalists. Computational propaganda is one of the most powerful new tools **against** democracy.[18]

According to Samuel C. Woolley and Philip N. Howard, authors of the working papers describing the results of the Oxford Internet Institute study, "Automated political communication involves the creation, transmission, and controlled mutation of significant political symbols over expansive social networks."[18] The case studies in their collection of working papers demonstrate the origins and very concrete consequences of computational propaganda, and they suggest as follows:

> It is time for social media firms to design for democracy….In the U.S., strategists are already planning for the 2018 mid-term elections. Let's assume that authoritarian governments will continue to use social media as a tool for political control. But for democracies, we should assume that encouraging people to vote is a good thing. Promoting political news and information from reputable outlets is crucial. Ultimately, designing for democracy, in systematic ways, will help restore trust in social media systems.
>
> Computational propaganda is now one of the most powerful tools against democracy. Social media firms may not be creating this nasty content, but they are the platform for it. They need to significantly redesign themselves if democracy is going to survive social media.[18]

How Our Brains Function Online

Why are so many engaged on social media? The National Academy of Sciences published a Harvard University study demonstrating that people enjoy sharing information about themselves with others and that "self-disclosure was strongly associated with increased activation in the brain regions that form the mesolimbic dopamine system...."[19] Dopamine is a chemical produced in the brain that is activated in response to pleasure. It is highly associated with addiction.

According to Eva Ritvo, M.D., a psychiatrist and vitality expert, in addition to dopamine, our brains secrete oxytocin, the "love hormone," when we empathize with others telling their stories. "Digging deeper into the mechanism, we find mirror neurons in the brain that are triggered when we see someone expressing emotions.... Emotions are contagious, and Facebook is a hotbed of positive emotions beckoning us to return for more. So, we do."[20]

Many believe social media may be changing our brains as well. Robert Epstein, a psychologist at The American Institute for Behavioral Research and Technology believes "Technologies are rapidly evolving that can impact people's behaviors, opinions, attitudes, beliefs on a massive scale—without their awareness."[21] I repeat, "...without their awareness"!

Guy P. Harrison asks, "Have some of us made a fool's bargain? Have we traded some of life's deepest rewards for fleeting and soon-forgotten micro-doses of dopamine?"[17]

Jaron Lanier, a technology expert and virtual reality pioneer goes so far as to advise "social media users to stop calling themselves 'users' because they are being 'used.'"[17]

In an inciteful article by Katy Steinmetz published in the August 26, 2018 issue of Time Magazine, Katy uses the subtitle "Bots and Propagandists are just Part of the Problem. The Bigger Issue is Your Brain."[22] In her article Katy reports on research conducted at Stanford University by psychologist Sam Wineburg in an effort to understand why even the smartest among us is so bad at making judgments about what to trust online. Among his findings, most of us fail to ask important questions about the content we encounter online before we read. Most importantly, we should be asking and ascertaining who or what is publishing this online information, and what bias or hidden agenda might have prompted them to write this information. Other studies show that people retweet links without even clicking on them to see what the link actual connects to. One study found that 6 in 10 links get retweeted without users' reading anything besides someone else's summation of the link results. Wineburg says (metaphorically), "We are all driving our [internet] cars, but none of us have licenses."[22] Steinmetz also reported that MIT cognitive scientist David Rand has found that "on average, people are inclined to believe false news at least 20% of the time."[22] Ouch!!

Steinmetz' article asserts "We don't fall for false news just because we're dumb. Often it's a matter of letting the wrong impulses take over."[22] Those impulses include first, not taking time to read beyond the headlines; second, allowing our desire for likes to supersede our gut feelings that a story might be dicey and questionable; and third, allowing political convictions to lead us to lazy thinking. False stories travel six times faster than true stories on Twitter, apparently because lies have better shock value. Falsehoods stir emotions of anger or disgust when they are recognized and sometimes affirmation when they are thought to be true. Unfortunately, in social interaction, humans would often rather be entertaining than correct, but these impulses spread fake news. David Rand, an MIT cognitive scientist, is quoted in Steinmetz' article as saying, "What makes the false or hyper-partisan claims do really well is they're a bit outlandish. That same thing that makes them successful in spreading online is the same thing that on reflection, would make you realize it wasn't true."[22] Katy writes, "But there is an even more fundamental impulse at play: our innate desire for an easy answer."[22]

Psychologists study cognitive shortcuts known as heuristics. These are the myriad ways we make decisions without having to analyze everything. Imagine how complicated getting the simplest of tasks done would be without taking shortcuts in thinking. House cleaning, yard work, cooking and grocery shopping would take forever, and we would be full of self-doubt about whether we were doing every little thing correctly and in the best way possible. Familiarity and exposure are two shortcuts (defined by heuristics) that lead us to believe or trust something. So, if we have already been exposed to a story, whether true or not, we are more likely to believe a similar story. If we are familiar with a person, we are likely to trust that person rather than question where their information came from. In fact, many people get their news from their friends on social media rather than from a reputable news outlet. This dangerous trend threatens truth and spreads false news. We must curb our own inclination to get news from our social group rather than trustworthy news organizations. Getting a heads up from our friends is okay, but it is a free thinker's responsibility to do the due diligence and verify what is true and trustworthy. Furthermore, we must recognize that our friends may simply be retweeting a link they haven't even checked out themselves. We must recognize that a retweet is not the same as an endorsement of belief. Much of what is shared on social media is shared just for entertainment value. Shortcuts are helpful in many tasks, but not in judging truthfulness.

Ironically, such shortcuts can backfire on us. According to Steinmetz, Pew researchers noted that "one reason people knowingly share made-up news is to 'call out' the stories as fake. That might make a post popular among like-minded peers on social media, but it can also help false claims sink into the collective consciousness."[22] Another problem related to lazy thinking was discovered when Facebook started warning that some posts contained material fact-checkers rated as false. Instead of simply accepting the help, people began believing anything that wasn't flagged must be true as they unconsciously implemented a mental shortcut.[22] If you want to avoid this accidental misstep, check out how fact-checkers analyze online information in Chapter (7) Seven.

In addition, we make incorrect assumptions about how the internet works. For example, many people assume that the higher something appears in your search results, the more reliable it is. Where a result appears has nothing to do with reliability. Search algorithms are based on keywords, not truthfulness. In fact, online propagandists know how to insert keywords into their content just so their story or blog, etc. appears higher up in your search results. Another incorrect assumption is the use of the size of others' followings as an indication of reliability. It is not, but based on the fact that people believe it is, many corporations, political organizations, and others will actually purchase followers in an effort to be believed. Visuals, too, are often automatically trusted, but photoshop and many apps have made this assumption also incorrect.

Some of the experts referenced in Katy Steinmetz' article believe the answer is in resisting snap judgments, and I agree that doing so will go a long way in protecting our free thinking. David Rand is quoted as saying, "It's not that people are being super-biased and using their reasoning ability to trick themselves into believing crazy stuff. It's just that people aren't stopping. They're rolling on."[22] In other words, they simply aren't taking the time to think critically and skeptically before reacting and sharing. This is most definitely a problem, so part of the solution is simply to stop and think. Yes, indeed, that is certainly necessary. But I believe knowledge is power, and a better understanding of the technology we are using will help us protect ourselves from the propaganda that is out there.

All this presents a worrisome situation and should light a fire under our butts to do what is necessary to protect our ability to think freely and clearly. So, what can we do? Self-education is a good start.

Understanding Bots, Sockpuppets, Trolls, and Catfishing

In order to understand what you can do to defend your ability to think freely, it is imperative you understand a little bit about how the internet and social media programs work. Which brings us to the problem of bots, botnets, and bot swarms. Social media, in particular, is infected with this cancer, and the prognosis for the patient is a continued decline in health.

The term bot is short for robot. On the internet bots are computer programs that perform tasks at a much higher rate than humans can. They often fake being real people and promote the interests and propaganda of the bot creator. Bots do many things, but free thinkers must be aware of one thing they do quite frequently: send false information and fake news to billions of people. Since some bots have machine-learning capability, they will adjust their message to appeal to you. Adrienne LaFrance writes in *The Atlantic*, "More than half of web traffic comes from automated programs—many of them malicious…. Overall, bots—good and bad—are responsible for over 52% of web traffic…."[23] And harmful bots were responsible for almost 30% of all web traffic. It is scary to think that much of our "social contact" on social media is with machines. Don't forget this important point. You can never be 100% certain who or what is on the other side of your screen. For the complete study from which this information is available and much more enlightening detail, Igal Zeifman's report is available online as of this writing.[24]

Bots can also act as trolls. Trolls are people who make it their mission to respond to others with ugly, disparaging remarks. For whatever reason, they will viciously attack someone for expressing an opinion or an idea with which they disagree. Emboldened by the fact that their victims cannot bloody their noses and physically defend themselves as was the case in the face-to-face bullying of yore, these online bullies act shamefully with no sense of constructive disagreement, honor or restraint. Some in their audience may find this entertaining, as if they are watching a soap opera play out through the words on the screen. But real people and our democracy are the victims of these malicious, uncivil attacks on free speech. Worse yet, bots have been programmed to implement coordinated harassment campaigns in place of trolls, who hide their cowardice or corruption behind the machinery and inhumanity of computer programs.

Botnets & Cyborgs

A botnet is a network of bots working in coordination. Often the result of this is a bot swarm, where many robotic computer programs work together to achieve a goal that would be difficult for individual bots to do on their own. A cyborg is part human, part automated bots. The human administers dozens of accounts. When a bot swarm implements a coordinated harassment campaign or fake news campaign, it appears as if thousands, maybe millions of people are all on board and in agreement with whatever the bot swarm is promoting. By itself, this is a form of propaganda.

Such a situation is a type of influence campaign that relies on the perception of popularity to get people to jump on the bandwagon. Other types of influence campaigns usually involve appealing to a user's confirmation bias using a variety of propaganda tools and the psychology of human needs such as those discussed in chapter one. In an influence campaign, truth is only important to the degree that it can be twisted to influence us, so it is up to each of us to avoid allowing ourselves to be sucked up into the vacuum created by combining truth, falsehood and propaganda.

Sockpuppets, Bot Farms & Trolls

Related to bots are sockpuppets. A sockpuppet account is created by one person who makes it appear as if someone else controls the account. When the someone else is a real person, the activities of the sockpuppet may be called *catfishing*. However, the "someone else" may be a fake persona, a made-up person. Note: Bots, themselves, can be programmed to act as real people, and they can take on stolen identities and fictional personalities, too. When bots are at least partially controlled by a human, the network may also be called a sockpuppet rather than a cyborg. Essentially, the sockpuppet human controls the bot farm. The human programmer takes the place of the machine-learning of one or more of the bots. He or she steps in to reprogram or direct bot responses to feedback the bots bring to the human. To use a military comparison, in Russia's cyberwars against America and other countries, their sockpuppets are the humans acting as the colonels in charge of a brigade of bots. Some of the bots themselves may act as lieutenant colonels; so, the human may not be directing everything, but only those things the bots cannot be programmed to do or those activities for which the human wants to be the decision-maker. More on Russian cyborgs later.

A note on trolls. Although bots can be programmed to act as trolls and can be said to be trolling (harassing), when we refer to trolls, we are usually referring to real humans not hiding behind bots or fake identities.

Welcome to our brave new cyber world. Perhaps we should have known it was coming, but more importantly, are we prepared to defend ourselves and keep our minds free to think clearly as we enjoy the benefits of social media and the internet. We have seen that our government is not defending us on social media. Should the government regulate social media in our defense? What about our children's defense? What about other parts of the internet? If we choose, we in a democracy can decide the answers by demanding more of our government and of the companies having power to make changes, but for the most part we are just beginning to understand the risks and dangers of our brave new cyber world. The luxury of passive cyber-use risks the demise of our freedom. If we are not able to think freely, we are not truly free. Propaganda has long been a tool of those who would control how and what we think. Social media has presented new and powerful opportunities for dictators, autocrats, and the power-crazed among us to practice social manipulation using mind games, propaganda, and other active measures developed over the past century.

How Russia is Rolling the Dice with Active Measures and Social Media

The GRU, once known as the KGB, Russia's spy and espionage agency, have become masters in population manipulation, and now social media has added to the powerful tools they have honed on East European countries. They have practiced population manipulation in Chechnya, Ukraine, Crimea, and on their own people for decades. Understanding how they work and what they do is essential in protecting ourselves from them and other authoritarian regimes (as well as American authoritarian politicians) that may one day be as sophisticated in such abilities. Regimes like China and North Korea have followed Russia's lead in developing active measures capability. Others may soon follow.

Active Measures

Active measures are a combination of techniques used over a long period of time to sow confusion, division, fear, and hate. Once people fall victim to these emotional and mental traps, they become vulnerable to suggestion and all the problems and challenges to free-thinking discussed in this book. Logic and truth are manipulated, twisted, and spun using active measures and making the individual's ability to harness their own logic ever more difficult since the truth is questioned, distorted, and refuted dishonestly.

Plausible Deniability

Plausible deniability is built into active measures so the Russians, and others implementing active measures, can offer some aspect of a specific scenario to try to coverup their involvement in perpetrating a bad act. By building plausible deniability into the bad act, the Russians are often successful in getting people to think, "Well, maybe it wasn't the Russians," or "I guess it could have been someone else." (Maybe a four-hundred-pound person somewhere in Romania as suggested by a candidate for President.) The doubt they cast leads many people to stay on the fence of uncertainty, instead of pursuing the truth despite Russian, or others', spin on the situation. Do not surrender your free thinking to anyone's spin on the situation. The Russians and many politicians are trying to get you to not be against them or find fault with them. They figure if you are not supportive, at least if you are not against them, they have one less detractor, and as such, you might as well be a supporter for all anyone else knows.

Here is one way plausible deniability works. The basics of it include combining falsehood with truth. The true side is used to promote the falsehood.

The Russians may use the psychology of greed, desire for fame, financial motives, or some other human weakness to manipulate a person to perform actions or divulge confidential information that makes this person appear guilty of some or all of the bad act perpetrated by the Russians. The Russians may then deflect their guilt onto the victim or use the victim to present plausible alternatives to the real facts. If a nation-state takes part in an action that can be used to place blame on a country or group, they will use this convenient circumstance to plausibly deny their responsibility. They use "whataboutisms" to promote doubt in our minds and to distract from the issue in question.   A whataboutism responds to allegations of wrong doing by asking "What about...?" and filling in the blank with a plausible concern that avoids the original issue in question. This is an attempt to deflect from the question or issue at hand and distract the listener, focusing his or her attention on some other concern. This works either because most of us want to be fair to all sides and consider all evidence or because we allow our confirmation bias to allow us to be persuaded. However, a whataboutism is not evidence. It is just distraction, and we must recognize it as just distraction. Consider only the evidence.

Russian bad actors deny involvement when they are the ones setting up the coercive situations leading to unwitting people and sometimes whole organizations playing into their hand and unknowingly supporting their propaganda or goals. An example of an organization being played by the Russians is the NRA.   The American National Rifle Association is suspected of being duped by a Russian operative, Maria Butina, whose arrest in July 2018 was authorized by a federal grand jury, is accused of conspiracy and acting as a foreign agent in her infiltration of the NRA. She is thought to have been working to get members of the NRA, knowingly or unknowingly, to serve the interests of the Russian government.

Russia is interested in influencing an audience and creating behavior change that supports and benefits their goals. They are playing the long game believing patience and persistence will pay off. They are correct in their assessment unless people are informed as to how they operate and unless all Americans and freedom-loving people around the world are alert to their tactics. This is so both on social media as well as in traditional media where they attempt to work their active measures too. How long can individuals tolerate the repetition of confusion and fear-mongering before they give up on trying to determine truth, and instead, simply follow a leader blindly? Each of us needs sufficient education to withstand the active measures, used by Russians and others, which we will likely be subjected to over the course of our lifetimes.

In all matters of importance, take the time to dig up the truth. This often entails not listening to the opinions of those who have self-interest in promoting a certain slant or side of an issue. It's essential to find the people you can trust that have the expertise needed to evaluate an issue with a clear head. By definition, that cannot be the same person for every issue. Your best friend, your brother, your aunt will have opinions, but not the expertise to make those opinions persuasive. Listen politely, but verify the truth and think for yourself.

Techniques of Russian Social Media Manipulation

In 2014, Clint Watts, a cybersecurity expert and author of *Messing with the Enemy,* began noticing a disturbing trend on the Twitter platform. In his words, "Twitter was increasingly a space where the angry, the disgruntled, and the unhappy unleashed their rage on the world. [He] had been trolled before, but these trolls…were relentless. Something was different about them."[25]

You guessed it. Clint was being subjected to the relentless heckling of Russian bots and sockpuppets often posing as anything but Russian. Although we know now that the Russian military is quite active in cyberwar and cyber manipulation, the Russians also use others to do their dirty work: Russian citizens, cyber enthusiasts in other countries, etc. This allows them to create and use plausible deniability to defend their government when accused of cyber-crimes and other corrupt activities.

Hecklers, Honeypots, and Hackers

Russian troll armies are effective because they use several methods of deception and they are persistent. I defined trolls as people who harass others with menacingly mean intent. Russian information trolls are a bit different. The Russian **hecklers** do bad-mouth and deride people on social media, but the intent is to win audience followers. They confirm the beliefs of those in their audience that support Russian goals, and they heckle or try to disparage those who oppose them. They target audiences they believe will be receptive to their ideas. Using wedge issues that divide and stir up emotions (such as civil war statues, flag-burning, immigration etc.), they then feed these target audiences their propaganda-filled perspective to hook them into the line of thinking that will benefit Russian goals. When they encounter adversaries, they focus the angst of their cultivated supporters against opposing messengers and their messages. They get others to join in the heckling. At times they are very sophisticated and coordinated, at other times they use very simple techniques.

According to Mr. Watts, hecklers are not about hacking people's computers, but about "hacking their minds, in two ways. In one sense, they [seek] to change a target audience's perception on issues, nudging audiences toward preferred foreign policy positions and influencing experts, politicians, and media personalities towards a...pro- Russian stance. When not shaping audience conversations through a barrage of slanted content and supporting banter, hecklers [seek] to batter adversaries off social media platforms through either endless harassment or compromise."[25]

Their success lies in their persistence and their pervasiveness. By employing bot swarms, mimicking humans, they amplify their messages. This gives their audience a false feeling of popularity for the idea being promoted by the Russians. Peer pressure is a persuasive propaganda technique that is easy to falsely create on social media by using bots and cyborgs. They don't give up easily. They are persistent. But if not successful with one audience, they will search out another and try again. (If at first you don't succeed....) They are pervasive. Clearly, the odds are in their favor. However, if heckling does not work, they have other tricks up their sleeves.

In the old world of espionage, a **honeypot** was an attractive woman who seduced information and cooperation out of unsuspecting men. Online honeypots may act in a similar manner, but not all online honeypots use this technique and not all online honeypots have female personas. In political and social issue arenas, a honeypot may be a strident supporter who woos your trust by his or her ardent support of your ideas, buttering-up a supposedly like-minded person who will soon be a victim. A person or bot acting as your political ally tries to win your trust and become your "close friend." If they can get close enough, they will try to manipulate information out of you that will allow them to break into your computer. They may request direct messaging capability so they can "share insights and secrets." In reality, clicking a link they may send you results in malware installation on your computer. Once in your computer, they look for "kompramat," compromising or embarrassing information which they then leak to discredit their victim. When a person is discredited, their ideas are discredited by association even when the "kompramat" has nothing to do with the issues and ideas being advocated by this person. Human nature is to focus on salacious information rather than the merits of ideas. Free thinkers should not fall for this propaganda technique. Consider first the merits of ideas rather than the human weaknesses of the messenger. After all, none of us is perfect.

If hecklers and honeypots are not successful, the troll army **hackers** can be called up to wage war on actual computers. In the Russian playbook, if the Kremlin disinformation squad cannot get you to tow the Kremlin line and think like a "good ole boy" or their version of the patriotic American, they will simply "take you out." Within their own country this may mean a sudden, mysterious disappearance, a poisoning with a rare substance, or outright murder on a city street. In the cyber world, however, your computer may suddenly be unable to access the internet. You will be disconnected from your social media feeds and accounts. Or worse, your personal computer or smart phone will be fried, melted into trash. The Kremlin does not accept "No" for an answer. This is how authoritarians work, and Russia is bringing their form of powerplay to America.

Persistent, Pervasive and Evolving Threats

It's important to recognize that the Russia playbook is not all-powerful. Though sophisticated, success is very often determined by the Russian willingness to persist and the pervasive nature of their online attacks as previously discussed. What we are also learning is that the Russians, and others using active measures, are willing to change and evolve and adapt their tactics as needed. To this end, Americans and others must be ever vigilant and supportive of those people and organizations among us that work to protect us. Ultimately, however, each individual must be persistently willing to defend themselves. Our guard must not be let down.

Recognizing Bot Activity on Social Media

Media Corporation operates a site, Data for Democracy, that can help you understand the internet threats to democracy and suggests ways we can defend ourselves. For myself, I simply don't get my news and information from social media but look for more reliable sources, which we will discuss in the next chapter. Each of us must decide for ourselves, and so I offer this information so you can make a more informed decision about your news and information sources.

Kris Shaffer, a data scientist and digital media specialist, along with Bill Fitzgerald, has published a web article titled "Spot the Bot: Identifying Automation and Disinformation on Social Media."[26] In this article they offer ways to identify whether information in your feed is coming from an automated or semi-automated source. They write, "With these signs, anyone can spot a bot, and resist the spread of disinformation online."[26]

Of course, to work, each of us must refrain from passing on information we do not absolutely know to be true, no matter what the source of that information is, even if it's your best friend or favorite uncle. If we want to pass on a tweet or a picture just because we find it funny, we should hesitate and cautiously consider how our intended audience will react. Are the persons cyber-savvy enough to recognize disinformation for themselves? Are the persons likely to irresponsibly pass the entertainment on as fact or without stating that it might not be true? Finally, if we do choose to pass it on, we have a duty to preface it with "NOT LIKELY TRUE, but so funny."

I found some of the suggestions made by Shaffer and Fitzgerald to be cumbersome, so I simply won't get the news I am willing to believe from social media, but you should decide for yourself how you will get your news and facts. The authors suggest a number of traits that admittedly are not foolproof. Individually, the traits may not indicate bots or sockpuppets. "None of them are foolproof," they write. "But the more of these traits an account displays, the more likely it is to be a disinformation account."[26]

Here is a synopsis of the traits identified by Shaffer and Fitzgerald at the website Medium.com/ Data-for-Democracy.

1.) **The account never sleeps**. If you download tweets [etc.] from a time period of several days, and there is no break in activity when a human would sleep, the account is automated to some extent.

2.) **Accounts that are exclusively retweets (or pretty close)** and exhibit some of the other traits listed here are likely to be part of a mass influence campaign. "Through sheer volume, retweet bots can function to amplify, normalize, and mainstream disinformation."[26]

3.) **Reply bots** are programmed to immediately reply to pre-loaded content. If every time you type certain words, text, hashtags or links, you get a response from a particular account, that account is likely automated and untrustworthy.

4.) **Stolen content** from other accounts will often be used by automated accounts intending to spread malware or collect user data. That stolen content may take the form of clickbait (content engineered to attract attention and convince high numbers of users to click on the link, which takes the user to an external site, typically, a hashtag related to a hot topic or an extremist community). Although these bots are simply trying to get ad revenue by getting you to click on their bait, the stolen clickbait content is also often the most polarizing and may overlap with another influence operation.

5.) **Stolen profile images and overly patriotic pictures or banner images** are associated with automated accounts. Performing a reverse image search, you will find this profile image is being used by other accounts exhibiting bot-like or sockpuppet-like features. "…[I]n our experience it seems that American flags, pictures of Donald Trump and the red 'Make America Great Again' baseball cap photo-shopped onto a celebrity are all far more common occurrences among false accounts than among real accounts."[26]

6.) **Tell-tale account names** are a good clue the account is automated. Artifacts of the automated account-creation process will often yield names that give clues. Such names may include variations on a single "real" name, variations on a celebrity name, and long strings of alphanumeric garbage (often after a "real" name).

7.) **Recent Accounts** or "young" accounts are prevalent in disinformation campaigns. Sometimes, however, older accounts are purchased for use in a botnet because they will appear less bot-like. In such cases, the previous account holder's activity will be deleted, so these accounts will show very recent initial activity if they are being used as a botnet.

8.) **Activity Gaps or Filler Content** often occur when the bot or sockpuppet is in between disinformation or influence campaigns. Filler content may be inserted between campaigns and is most commonly either inspirational quotations or pornography.

9.) **Timing:** If suddenly the news is reporting huge numbers of accounts responding with the same hashtag such as when in January, 2018 #releasethememo flooded the internet, it could easily have botnets involved.

It is impossible for the average user to know, but if the hashtag is related to a political or social issue, it could have and likely has a botnet involved. Don't be fooled by this appearance of unity or popularity—not that a free-thinking individual would be influenced merely by this appearance.

10.)**Semantic Similarity** is the use of similar wording from one account to another. When exact repetition occurs across multiple social media platforms, it is a clear sign of large scale coordination. Some perpetrators may be coordinating and reproducing language from a shared script. In this case text may be very similar, if not exact, while the images will likely be the same.

It is important to note again that most of the traits listed above do not conclusively indicate bot or sockpuppet activity. However, when an account exhibits two or more of these traits, it's definitely time to be skeptical about the source. The account most likely involves machines and not just an individual account user. Whoever is behind the bot or botnet is running an influence campaign, and that campaign is likely filled with propaganda, disinformation, and hype.

Why America and Free Societies are Vulnerable to SM Manipulation

Americans have worried most about infrastructure attacks and attacks on the structural components of our elections system. Reasonable people should worry about this and take actions to defend these vulnerable and critical aspects of our society. But the more important cyberwar is the information control and manipulation the Russians are so good at implementing. And SM (social media) platforms have made it so much easier for the Russians and other bad actors to manipulate us. The war for American minds and hearts is serious and threatens democratic values and democracy itself. Furthermore, our free and open society, and the very values democracy is based on, make us and other liberal democratic countries most vulnerable to this type of cyber warfare. What is our strength is also our vulnerability—a weakness for adversaries to use against us.

Russia recognizes this and intends to use it to their advantage. And we must recognize that to protect our democracy, we must all be able to protect our free thinking, and that means we must know and understand the threats we face. The war will not be in some far-off land, rather it will be right here in our communities, our households, on our computers, smart phones, future technology, and in our own minds. We must be willing and ready to fight for our freedom, the freedom of our ability to think and to determine truth.

Free speech allows everyone to say and write almost anything— true or false. Because of this, if we cannot recognize or determine falsehoods, we will be victims of lies and distortions. Common sense cannot protect us from the barrage of falsehoods and devious reasoning we will encounter. Neither can legislation without in some way reducing our freedom. This means our freedom will be determined by our ability to recognize active measures by our enemies, both foreign and domestic, and other forms of information warfare both on social media and within more traditional media.

Defending Your Ability to Think Clearly on Social Media

Although social media presents new challenges to free thinking citizens, the basic awareness and understanding of techniques of propaganda, Maslow's Hierarchy of Needs, and confirmation bias are the most important tools free thinkers have to defend themselves. Being aware and skeptical of what you are presented with on the internet is a healthy habit. Don't be one to jump on the bandwagon. Instead, look for reliable sources of information and always be willing to listen to the other side of the issue. Find out the real facts and verify, verify, verify before making a final decision. Very importantly, don't be part of the echo chamber and part of the problem by forwarding unverified information. This is not just irresponsible, but in some circumstances would be unpatriotic.

Social and Cultural Changes to Promote Free Thinking on Social Media

Citizens must care about and value truth over the entertainment value of falsehood, conspiracy theory, and manipulated facts. When making decisions, especially political decisions, individuals must demand correct information. The health of our democracy must not be taken for granted. It is perhaps as important as our own personal health. This is what we hope to pass on to our children and grandchildren, and for this reason we must take care of it. We must all demand correct information unvarnished with bias and opinion. Only after considering unvarnished truth should we entertain people's opinions.

It starts with adequate curriculum in our schools. Students must be sufficiently taught to recognize propaganda and avoid falling for misinformation. Parents and society must demand and insure our schools are doing the best job possible in this regard. Democracy depends on it.

We all must not only be willing to self-educate, but to recognize and question our own prejudices. It isn't easy to acknowledge when we are believing something for which we have few or maybe no facts— but this is what responsible adults must teach themselves to do. And we must foster this critical thinking skill in our school children. Ultimately, we must be willing to correct beliefs that are not based on fact.

These personal traits are not easy to implement consistently. Tribalism and confirmation bias are strong-willed culprits to overcome, and the two lurk within

us all. For this reason, an equally powerful tool is recommended by some: shame.
Should we make sharing disinformation and falsehoods as shameful as drunk
driving?   I would argue, yes, the dangers to our freedom from online
misinformation is so great. We cannot risk the death of democracy from social
media's impact on our ability to think freely. Psychologist Sam Wineburg insists
we must promote an awareness of "digital pollution" on the Internet. "We have to
get people to think that they are littering by forwarding stuff that isn't true."[22]
Echoing our American founding fathers, Katy Steinmetz adds, "Having a well-
informed citizenry may be, in the big picture, as important to survival as having
clean air and water."[22]

Chapter 7

Real News or Fake News

How can we tell fact from fiction?

Let's face it. Discerning fact from fiction is not as easy as one would think. We have our internal desire for confirmation biasing our judgement, not to mention other aspects of our human nature attempting to interfere with our clear thinking. We want to believe what we want to believe. That is our first challenge, and we have discussed at length how to recognize when we are our own worst enemies in the search for the truth. Correcting that obstacle to free thinking takes determination and practice. The modern media environment presents new challenges of its own requiring determination and practice to differentiate truth from the other noise and avoid spreading false information.

Although traditional news sources such as *The Wall Street Journal, The New York Times, The Washington Post*, and other large urban newspapers have fallen into disfavor, their journalists are schooled in standards of journalism that have been developed over decades. These are standards that many non-traditional sources of news and information may not abide by. Are these standards foolproof? No. To the extent that news and information is coming from humans, there will always be the potential for human error, but would you rather have an internet bot tell you what's up.

Historical Perspective

It helps to have a strong understanding of press history. We all know that the Founding Fathers of America put in place a set of checks and balances to prevent the corrupting influence that power often has on leaders, and other democracies have followed suit. All healthy democracies adhere to the principle of freedom of the press and presume that citizens will figure out what is fact and what is fiction. Today, the threat of an autocrat in the Presidency is what was then the threat of a monarch. The Founding Fathers, were not satisfied that government checks and balances were enough to prevent a return to monarchical rule, so they devised the Bill of Rights and established the people's right to a free press. Our hope of avoiding an autocratic ruler still lies in the Constitutional Amendments within the Bill of Rights and, in particular, the successful operation of our free press. I would argue that despite its shortcomings, the free press is the best tool citizens have to curb corruption in their government. It is stronger even than the balance of power between the three branches of government. The reason it is so powerful is that as a whole, it does not cater to any one particular group or party.

The job of our free press is to be our eyes and ears, our watchdog, over our government so that we, the people, can have power over our government and continue to live under the rule of democratic principles. Having a diverse free press makes this possible. Indeed, the greatest threat to this important aspect of democracy is when media businesses grow too big and begin to exercise monopoly power in any domain. It is simply not possible to have a democracy without a free and diverse press.

The Fairness Doctrine

Because the press is not part of government, but a business, it suffers the pressures of surviving in what might seem like a dog-eat-dog competitive business environment. To this end headlines are often outlandish and sometimes misleading. And it is because of this that some (maybe too many) pander to what their audience wants to hear rather than sticking to just the facts. To help avoid biased reporting, America established *The Fairness Doctrine* was established in

1949. It required equal airtime for differing points of view. It is the reason the State of the Union address by the President is now followed by a speech from the opposing party, so that listeners have an opportunity to weigh opposing perspectives. Most living today cannot imagine it any other way. Unfortunately, under the Reagan administration, the Federal Communications Commission abolished *The Fairness Doctrine* in 1987. This was a government regulation that helped Americans understand more than one side of many issues and seemed to truly serve the good of the people. Did the Reagan administration have the support of the American people when the doctrine was abolished? Did citizens drop the ball and allow an ideological anti-government sentiment to hurt rather than help further our democracy? (We are reminded that some government is good government and lack of any government is chaos and anarchy. In other words, although too much government may not be good, some government regulations are needed and helpful. Moderate balance is sometimes the best option.) Up until this change, American citizens were generally very confident in both newspapers and television news. That confidence increasingly diminished when only one side of an issue was presented.

After the Fairness Doctrine: Talk Radio, Cable TV & SM

After the abolishment of the Fairness Doctrine, the media landscape began changing dramatically. First, biased talk radio shows began presenting one-sided opinions. The respected journalist Dan Rather writes, "For hours on end, [these shows] would present their view of the world without rebuttal, fact-checking, or any of the other standards in place at most journalistic outlets. Often their commentary included bashing any media coverage that conflicted with the talk radio narrative."[27] Using vilification and other propaganda techniques, these shows built a clientele that basked in trash-talk and confirmation bias. Following this change in the media landscape came cable television and the rise of 24/7 news networks. To fill the time, these networks bring in pundits to give their opinions about current reporting—some also engage in trash-talk and promote confirmation bias, a few are actual experts, the one's to whom we should be listening. Then the dawn of internet news and social media allowed anybody to get into the business of disseminating news. Many of these internet sources have no standards other than getting users to click so the website can earn ad revenue. (How websites make money is covered in chapter 6 Social Media.)

The Free Press is Not Free

Despite these huge changes in the media landscape, Dan Rather calls the free press "an insurance policy for the continued health of the republic," and he makes the point that although it is the only business protected specifically in our Constitution, it operates in the service of us all.[27] I believe it is our right to have it, and it is our duty to protect its functioning so that it serves us. To do so, we must understand the basics, and we must vote with our dollars for those news sources we trust and want to use. Reality check: The free press is not free. Reputable investigative journalism—the kind needed to protect a democracy—not only is costly, but it must be guarded and supported by the citizens it serves to be strong and viable. We must each do our part. In fact, I recommend doing what I do. I treat my favorite investigative journalism companies as charities. I pay monthly for a subscription and think of it as a donation for the cause of protecting the democracy. I must admit I don't always have time to read or listen to these news sources, but I feel better knowing I am doing my part to make sure they are there when I need them.

What Fake News is Not

Fake news has recently received a great deal of attention, as it should, but fake news has been around for as long as fake doctors have been selling fake potions and fake ministers have been taking donations for fake religious organizations. There will, most likely, always be people attempting to defraud others for their own gain, whether it be for monetary, political, or some other personal benefit.

It's important to understand that fake news is not the same as erroneous or mistaken news reporting. Humans will make mistakes, but reputable organizations will acknowledge and set the record straight when they do. It's also important to recognize that there are times when reporters are manipulated or even duped by their sources. Reputable news organizations have checks in place to prevent incorrect information from being published, but even the best in the industry will have to publish a correction now and then. Most importantly, a person's misunderstanding of the news does not make the news fake. I taught my students this mantra, "Clarify and verify." Clarify to make sure you have understood the intended meaning of what you heard before you pass on information or base decisions on it, and verify the truth by consulting other reputable sources. We all must become adept readers and attentive listeners. As adult citizens, it is on us to maintain these skills that are critical to democracy. We must, as well, insure that our children become strong and proficient in these skills and recognize what their responsibilities will be as adults in a democracy. It is also on us to determine whether or not we are fully understanding news and information. If not, it's on us to seek clarification and complete understanding. Using more than one source for your news and information can help with this. Also, many reporters maintain blogs where you can ask questions to make sure you understood the report as intended.

What Fake News Is

Fake news can be defined as news fabrication deliberately designed to mislead and misinform, often as part of an influence campaign, but perhaps just as often a purely money-making venture. It may take the form of exaggeration, omission, untrue details or interpretation, out of context quotations, untrue quotations, doctored photographs with untrue captions, and propaganda. Tabloid newspapers, such as *The National Enquirer*, are less popular now that we can get tabloid and fake news online. In their heyday, and still, people would give money to read about the birth of a half human-half cheetah child destined to compete in the Olympics, and so on. If you are willing to be duped, you will be. The scary thought is that there are those out there that actually believe some of this trash.

Online fake news can also be outlandish. These campaigns love to promote conspiracy theories as truth. (In fact, some politicians and talk show hosts promote conspiracy theories as a form of fear propaganda.) Online fake news also tends to be aggressive and mean-spirited, using photoshopped pictures and crude, vulgar, or exaggerated language in their claims. However, if part of an influence campaign, the language might be much more subtle, and the fact that it is an outlandish claim might be difficult to determine.

It has been noted that many radio talk show hosts, though not all, regularly practice the distortion of fact and promotion of fantasy conspiracy stories and false conjecture. This is true of online media sources as well. This business model has worked simply because so many people are willing to tune in and perhaps believe despite little or no evidence being presented. Apparently, many are willing to be brainwashed as they sit in their cars driving to work or the grocery store. Yet another sad fact is that people like to have their emotions stirred up and are willing to listen to get the zingy high this creates. It's addictive. Yes, it may be entertaining, but allowing your brain to be bathed in the bull is an unhealthy threat to your free-thinking and ultimately unhealthy for democracy. The radio stations and the talk show hosts are most interested in their bottom line and profits, not promoting democracy. They play heavily to the confirmation bias of their audience, and it works. Listen to some fun music, instead.

Social Media News

And then there is social media news. Research shows that on social media people tend to believe stories based on who shares the story with them rather than the facts and evidence behind the story. In 2016, intelligent people and politicians, who should automatically exercise caution and double-check what are believed to be facts, were fooled. In an NBC online news article by Ben Popken, it was reported that at least forty celebrities and politicians retweeted or engaged with accounts created by a Russian troll factory…. "Over 3,000 global news outlets also inadvertently published articles containing embedded tweets by the confirmed Kremlin-linked troll accounts in over 11,000 news articles in the run-up to the 2016 elections. Twitter has provided over 2,700 handles linked to the Internet Research Agency (IRA), a Russian intelligence agency-linked firm based in St. Petersburg, Russia."[28] The FBI, CIA, and NSA have all confirmed that Russians were conducting influence and misinformation campaigns to influence the United States' election. We now also know that,

> "during the 2016 presidential election: Russian intelligence agencies funded 'troll farms' that spread paid ads across Facebook and invented 'American' Facebook profiles to pass on fake news. Russian agents disseminated disinformation across Google as well,

<blockquote>including via its subsidiary YouTube, and through advertising on Google search, Gmail, and the company's DoubleClick ad network.[30]</blockquote>

Obviously, many people with good reputations accidentally helped the Russians spread their fake news. Double check even people you think you can trust. Oftentimes, trustworthy people don't know they have been duped. Furthermore, messages online can proliferate exponentially and virtually instantly, before fact-checking is done. And as covered in Chapter 6, social media is capable of micro-targeting literally anyone. Once information goes out as news, correcting the record on social media is next to impossible. Worse yet, if we allow our emotions and confirmation bias to buy into the falsehoods, we are part of making social changes based on deceit and propaganda. We are part of the disinformation campaigns being promoted by those with subversive intentions. We are part of the problem. With respect to Russian propaganda campaigns, it is commonly understood that their intent is to sow confusion and distrust so that people are unsure what to believe and unclear about what to do. This leads to a type of social paralysis during which a powerful and cunning leader can take almost total control of society, as Hitler did in the 1930s and '40s. The stakes are high.

"A New York Times examination of hundreds of [Russian] posts shows that one of the most powerful weapons that Russian agents used to reshape U.S. politics was the anger, passion and misinformation that real Americans were broadcasting across social media platforms."[30] Citizens make themselves part of the problem by spreading emotionally charged misinformation on social media. It bears repeating: "Think Before You Like."[15]

It is all too easy for news sources, especially those online, to confuse, mislead, and convince us of their garbage. We must take responsibility for determining the truth before we share. Otherwise, we become a tool in an online campaign to undermine our democracy, our free thinking, and our way of life. To be able to prevent this, we all must have basic understandings of the press and television news as well as all the previous information presented in this book.

Fact versus Opinion

It seems so obvious but ask yourself if your definition of fact versus opinion would help a fifth- grader understand the difference. If you are not sure, this section will be helpful. Nowadays, cable "news" programs are a mix of both. However, the majority of these so-called news programs are really analysis and commentary (opinion) of the news. Often the pundits interviewed serve the program's bias and agenda. So, as of this writing, MSNBC is thought to lean very left while Fox is thought to lean very right. Most other channels fall somewhere between those. Public broadcasting has generally been considered the least biased, although both the right and left will complain about public broadcasting to confuse us about the matter. If you have the time to witness first hand what is happening on the floor of Congress, you can watch C-SPAN. But C-SPAN, at times, also conducts interviews with pundits who spin their opinions rather than simply present facts. Remember, if you only watch one show, you are not getting a balanced and unbiased assessment and you are likely subjecting yourself to brainwashing.

Here is one way bias is projected through the media. Often, the primary moderator announces a fact or two and then turns to a guest or another moderator to ask their opinion. Their question may not indicate that they are asking for an opinion and not facts. For example, the moderator may ask, "What does all this mean?" More than likely the answer to that type of question is mostly interpretation (opinion); although additional facts may be sprinkled into the discussion. The viewer must determine what is fact and what is opinion and have the discipline to treat each appropriately. It would be irresponsible to pass opinions on as if they were facts. Most importantly, the viewer must determine what needs to be verified and what needs to be ignored until all the facts are verified. A reminder—when we hear an opinion that agrees with our beliefs, our confirmation bias kicks in, and we tend not to question or verify the facts offered as evidence. We are not thinking freely in this instance; we are brainwashed.

Definition of Fact

So how do we know what is fact? We cannot rely on the pundits, who are paid for their opinions, to tell us. Sometimes pundits will say "It's a fact…" when their comments are really only opinions. We must be able to know for ourselves. Let's begin with the definition of a fact. First, a fact is indisputable. There is no such thing as "alternative facts." If there can be an alternative, then the fact is not known and the conjectures or ideas are still in the realm of opinion. However, many pundits will offer alternatives to real facts to confuse you and make you think the facts are still in question. This is micro-brainwashing. They want you to believe their "alternative facts" so you will be on their side. We must choose to be on the side of truth and the side of our country's democracy, no matter how much we would rather believe alternatives. We must get off the bandwagon of belief and determine reality for ourselves.

Determining Facts

Facts can be verified and that is how you know they are facts. Keep skepticism in your mind until you are able to verify whether a fact is true. Falsehoods abound and "alternative facts" are likely just disinformation, a fancy word for lies, distortion, and exaggeration. Opinions, unlike facts, are strictly the person's personal ideas on a matter. Opinions are just beliefs. Some opinions are beliefs which may turn out to be factual but are not yet verified. Be aware that far too many cable programs are mostly about personal beliefs, not news. What else can they fill the 24-hour day with? There is plenty of news, but apparently, presenting only news would not captivate an audience. It is the free-thinking citizen's job to be skeptical and to verify before believing.

There are three basic ways to verify what is fact. First, you can either see it for yourself or take the word of an eye witness you trust. Whether a new car is red or blue will be determined by your eyesight. Whether a new car is red or burgundy will be determined by your eyesight, but it may also be determined by your definition of what the difference is between red and burgundy, so disagreement over this fact is really a disagreement over definition or semantics (word choice). If you find yourself on different sides of such a matter, it is only fair to acknowledge each side is using a different definition of the same fact in question. Is one side wrong? Are both sides right? This is where people start playing politics with the truth, so this is where consulting an unbiased expert would be the wise solution. Perhaps based on definition, we might agree to disagree in some instances, but this is not to say there is an alternative fact here. The color of the car remains the same.

Whether an Olympic athlete jumped higher or longer than another athlete will be measured or counted. Definition or semantics will have no bearing on the outcome. Counting or measuring is usually a very reliable method of determining certain facts. However, as explained in the section on availability bias in Chapter Five, numbers can sometimes be misinterpreted. This is also true in statistics where sample sizes are used to extrapolate a count and an actual count is not taken. So, with counting and measuring, it is still important to verify.

A third accepted way to verify facts is to gather evidence until a preponderance of evidence indicates whether something is likely to be true. This is the way our judicial system determines guilt versus innocence. As we know, it is not foolproof. This is also the way scientists determine findings even when eyesight and measuring are used. Note that scientists are held to a much higher standard for finding truth. They must apply all three methods. Also note that online our eyesight is not reliable. Pictures will be photoshopped by unscrupulous people. Always be skeptical of photographs. Finally, know that determining facts is not foolproof; therefore, it is our job to demand enough trustworthy evidence so that we can be sure of the facts. Verify, verify, verify.

For illustration, let's look at a hypothetical dialogue on a hypothetical cable channel news program.

> **Primary Moderator:**
> Fact: The President claims the crowd at his inauguration was the largest ever.
> Fact: It has been proven that the crowds attending his inauguration were not the largest ever.
> **Guests:**
> Opinion: The President is simply exaggerating which is not really a lie.
> Opinion: The President is exaggerating to make his base voters happy and proud. He said this "tongue in cheek."
> In other words, he was joking.
> Opinion: The president really meant that his digital crowd plus attendees made for the largest crowd ever.

Note first that each sentence is presented as if it were a fact. None were prefaced with "It is my opinion that." This is the first challenge. People most often do not announce when what they are saying is an opinion. Furthermore, people often believe that what they are saying is fact when it is only opinion. You must be the arbiter of true facts.

Next, notice that the two facts presented can be determined by counting and measuring the crowd size. So, these facts can be easily verified. The question that should come into a free-thinking person's mind is, "Has the crowd size actually been counted or measured?" On the other hand, the opinions cannot be verified for several reasons. First, the commentator acts as if he/she knows what another person (the President) is thinking. If this cannot be verified, it should not be accepted as fact. And remember, the fact that someone thinks something does not make what he/she thinks an actual fact. Second, whether or not exaggeration equals a lie is a matter of one's definition, not a matter of fact. (I usually consider exaggeration a lie, a form of propaganda, and unacceptable.) If it cannot be verified, it should not be claimed a fact nor accepted as a fact. Third, the motivation of another person cannot be known unless that person verifies it, so it is opinion as to what the motivation of the President is in this case. Finally, in the last opinion expressed, there are problems of whether or not digital crowd size can and has been counted. No evidence has been given. This opinion also acts as if the commentator knows what was being referred to when the President spoke. Again, we have no way of knowing if this is true without the President, himself, verifying this. Finally, remember a photograph in this situation is of limited use. Photographs can be doctored and used to make false claims.

We must practice recognizing these problems in both what we hear and see on television and what we read and see online. Moreover, there are other factors that should be considered when determining whether you should be skeptical about what is presented as fact.

Reputation & Bias

Who is the person presenting the facts and opinions? Does this person have a reputation for honesty? Does this person have an agenda, a personal benefit from representing a particular viewpoint or bias? Who does this person work for? What are this person's financial interests? Who is buttering his/her bread? What are this person's ideologies and political leanings? The answers to these questions will reveal if this person may tend to twist the truth to look differently than the simple facts might look. This is called expressing a bias. When a bias is verbally expressed it distorts the truth and may confuse listeners and readers. Although a bias is not necessarily intended to misinform, it usually is not the whole truth. Recognizing a bias is the first step in avoiding the brainwashing to which it may contribute. Most people are not neutral, so we must take this into account. Again, we must avoid accepting as fact ideas that simply support our current beliefs (confirmation bias). Instead, we must verify, verify, verify.

One website evaluating the bias of news organizations, websites, and specific news stories is Media Bias/Fact Check. This independent online media outlet publishes its methodology, funding, and a great deal of other information to help you determine whether you will trust its assessments. Ultimately, it will be our personal assessment that counts, but knowing how and why others have determined bias can be helpful. Just make sure your assessments are not influenced by your confirmation bias. Ask yourself, is the methodology sound and as objective as possible. Judgement is a necessary part of much of what humans do, but is the judgement based on fact rather than unsubstantiated belief. And, of course, verify, verify, verify.

Your Responsibility in Determining Facts

In determining fact versus fake fact from our news sources, we must use different methods because most of us are not on location to check for facts by looking around and counting. Instead, we will have to do three things. First, evaluate the source. Does it have a good reputation over a long period of time, and does it adhere to established standards of journalism—including admitting up front and openly when mistakes are made in their reporting. Second, determine if other reputable sources are reporting the same fact. Third, wait a day or two or more to make sure a mistake in reporting the purported fact does not have to be retracted.

Choosing a Trustworthy News Source

Reputable news sources do several things non-reputable sources do not do. They adhere to journalistic standards, which citizens should demand of all their news sources. These standards or best practices were established to prevent errors and fake news. Free speech, however, is still the law of the land, and there are many that do not try to prevent or correct errors. Journalistic standards have been honed over at least a century of reporting, and many of the most reputable news organizations have been in business for as long a time, in part because they have a good reputation and adhering to strict journalistic standards has served them well. That does not mean they never make mistakes. They do. All do. Verify. Verify. Verify.

Journalism Standards and Best Practices Basics

Look for these standards being practiced when evaluating your news sources for print, radio, television, and online journalism. If your news sources are not adhering to these standards, be skeptical and look for more reliable sources of news.

1. All facts should be confirmed by two or more reliable sources. One may be other news organizations, but one should be named and, on the record, which means the source is willing to be named and quoted. (As a news consumer, be aware that primary sources, sources with direct experience and

knowledge are much more reliable than secondary sources, which may provide hearsay. "So and so told me that…" is much less reliable and can be used to manipulate information.) The only time fewer than two reliable sources are allowed is when there are legal constraints, privacy issues or likelihood of danger.

2. Reporters should be required to convince their editors that the sources are trustworthy and the facts are correct. Reporters and editors must judge if the source has an agenda or bias and they are required to disclose this information. They won't write, "So and so has an agenda." Instead, they will tell you something about the person such as that he/she has a financial interest or works for a certain company. You have to recognize the potential for bias.

3. Reporters should not simply copy and paste from the newswires (organizations that share their news with other news organizations for pay). If this rule is broken because of the importance of getting the information out such as natural disasters, crime sprees, etc., the reporter must

    1.) Have evidence it happened,

    2.) Add the words "according to the wires" or something similar, and

    3.) Allow a senior editor to make the call whether to publish or not.

Under these circumstances verification usually takes place either by sending a reporter to the scene or by contacting victims or those affected and involved.

4. So that they can prevent reporting misinformation, reporters and editors should be expected to look for signs a source may be trying to manipulate them or distorting facts.

5. Quotations should be required to have context so that the reader or listener gets a clear understanding of what the speaker being quoted meant. Note to reader: Quotations out of context are used in disinformation and propaganda campaigns and should be ignored, due to confirmation bias, until context is obtained. Context being whatever else was said in the conversation by all persons involved and any background information.

6. Mistakes must be corrected as soon as they become known using a method that makes it clear to the reader or listener both what the mistake was and what the correction is. Note: Not correcting mistakes is a clear sign of disregard for truth and may indicate the "mistakes" were a deliberate part of an influence campaign. Best to ditch such a news source.

These are some of the basic standards used to achieve truth in journalism. There are others particular to the type of story being published, but beyond the scope of this handbook. A cautionary reminder is in order. If your news sources are adhering to standards that are less than those listed here, be skeptical. Even if your news sources are strictly adhering to these standards, verify, verify, verify. It is so important to have more than one source of news.

Non-reputable News Sources

With the dawn of internet news and the ease of reaching billions of people, thousands of self-proclaimed news websites are available. Many of these sites are simply not trustworthy and should be avoided. Many of them make their money by getting you to click on advertising links. And many will publish audacious claims to get you to click. Some of these sites are obviously tabloid or yellow journalism. (Yellow journalism and the yellow press are American terms for journalism and associated newspapers that present little or no legitimate, well-researched news while instead using eye-catching headlines for increased sales.

Techniques may include exaggerations of news events, scandal-mongering, or sensationalism.) Some are mean-spirited, preying upon our curiosity and voyeuristic tendencies. They publish gossip rather than news and are willing to publish when paid to do so. Sometimes, they will buy the exclusive rights to a story and then not publish. This is called "catch and kill." Catching a story and killing it is done to deliberately withhold information from the public. Sites that do this have an agenda. A story may be killed because it has incriminating or embarrassing information about someone they wish to protect. The motivations to catch and kill are many. These sites are likely involved in a disinformation campaign that benefits them either financially or politically. A site may be getting paid to withhold a story by a person who would be embarrassed by the publication of it. One could think of this as a form of extortion or a form of bribery. Corruption is not a stranger to business, even the news business.

There is simply too much bogus information on the internet, but perhaps that is the price of freedom of speech. MediaBiasFactCheck.com lists over 400 sites as "may be very untrustworthy and should be fact checked on a per article basis."[31] Free-thinking citizens must accept the responsibility of discerning the true from the bogus. These sites may publish some real news, but that is not their main concern. They need your clicks to make their money. They are not making money from news; however, publishing real news now and then may get someone to believe they are trustworthy and click for them. $Ka-ching!

Professional Fact Checkers

Nowadays, there are pros at many reputable news organizations that are paid to verify, verify, verify. It never hurts to take a few tips from the pros. What do professional fact-checkers do? First, they determine where information is coming from BEFORE reading it. (Confirmation bias makes it necessary to look first for the source.) Fact checkers almost always open a new tab and search what the web has to say about the person or organization sponsoring the site or article in question **before** they begin reading the site information. If a person never leaves a site, he/she is essentially allowing the site to stand behind a smokescreen of authenticity. You might as well let them put a hook in your nose. Your caught. Second, fact checkers also look immediately for additional sources of information on the same subject. They then compare each source's references side by side to determine which is the more reliable based on credentials and other feedback. Third, they do not trust what a site tells them about itself. They look elsewhere for that information. In other words, they find other sites that are not part of the source site to learn whether or not the source has a bias or agenda in presenting the information. Fourth, they exercise "click-restraint" by reviewing at least two pages of search results before deciding which they feel they can trust and therefore, which they will read. Rather than lazily clicking on the first thing they see, they understand how the web can by manipulated so that more reliable sites get buried. Fact checkers know that people or organizations with an agenda, a purpose other than getting at the truth, can game search results and pack their sites with keywords, so that their sites pop up first in response to an internet search.

Whether you practice all the techniques of a fact-checker, at minimum you should always ask and answer these two questions: Who or what is behind the information, and do they have a bias or agenda?

There are several fact-checking organizations sponsoring websites and The New York Times and The Washington Post have their own fact-checkers. A few sources I consider reputable include the following: FactCheck.org, Politifact.com, The Sunlight Foundation, MediaBiasFactCheck.com, and OpenSecrets.org.

Summary

The Internet Age has brought individuals immense access to information with the ability to educate and help ourselves to knowledge. Unfortunately, the Internet Age has also opened the doors of access to unscrupulous people who have their diabolical reasons to provide false and misleading information. It's very difficult to determine who or what institutions we can trust both on the internet and in print journalism. When we cannot be certain, it is best to go back to news sources we know adhere to traditional standards of news reporting. Using fact-checking websites may be helpful if we take the time this requires. The recommendation of this author is to seek reputable news organizations first then determine if the news in question comes from trustworthy sources. Next, determine if several trustworthy news organizations are reporting the same facts. Be skeptical and never pass on information as true and factual until you have waited at least a few days to insure the reporting is accurate. Verify, verify, verify.

In addition, do not let your confirmation bias or your use of only one news source cause you to believe what is not true. Recognize verifiable facts versus opinion. And be aware of how people use propaganda techniques to convince you of their "alternatives" and distortions.

Verify. Verify. Verify.

Chapter 8

Logical Fallacy or Fake Argument

In the old days debate was standard fair in most high school curriculum. If you had the opportunity to train for a debate under the guidance of a good teacher, you know that arguments can be made based on illogical connections. These arguments are called fallacies (mistakes) and are described as fallacious. In other words, they are errors in reasoning and, therefore, wrong. A logical fallacy is a mistake in logic. Many conspiracy theories use fallacy and fallacious connections between unconnected events in an attempt to substantiate the theory. Such arguments, on close scrutiny, simply don't make sense. However, "Beware the Jabberwock." Without a careful look, one can be fooled by these fake arguments. At first glance they seem to express a logic of a sort. In fact, fallacious arguments are not logical at all, and the free-thinking citizen must be able to recognize these weaknesses so as not to be brainwashed by "logical" fallacy, an oxymoron at best.

There are fifteen fallacious arguments described here. The last four are related to propaganda techniques discussed in chapter 3, and so may sound familiar. Information explaining these fallacies was gleaned from the University of North Carolina at Chapel Hill (UNC) which has produced a stellar webpage on the recognition of fallacies in writing as part of *The Writing Center*, an online resource. According to their website, "It is important to realize two things about fallacies: first, fallacious arguments are very, very common and can be quite persuasive, at least to the casual reader or listener. You can find dozens of examples of fallacious reasoning in newspapers, advertisements, and other sources. Second, it is sometimes hard to evaluate whether an argument is fallacious...An argument that has several stages or parts might have some strong sections and some weak ones."[32] With that, it can clearly be understood that an ability to recognize logical fallacy is another tool in the free thinker's toolbox.

False Cause Fallacy

This fallacy is one of the easier ones to catch. When an argument is made that B was caused by A simply because A came before B, you have a fallacy. For B to be proven as caused by A there must be other reasons. Simply having one thing come before the other does not indicate a cause. If the green car runs through the red light and then the blue car runs the red light, it does not mean that the accident the blue car had with the white car was caused by the green car. One thing coming before the other does not show cause. Although it is true that a cause comes before its effect, the time sequence of two or more events is not usually the reason one event may cause another. So, the cause of the accident with the white car was at least partly that the blue car ran the red light. The cause has nothing to do with the green car.

Slippery Slope Fallacy

In this fallacy a person will argue that a chain of events will occur if the first event occurs. Often the claimed result will be calamitous and it instills fear (a propaganda tool). The claim is that just one step onto the "slippery slope" will cause us to slide all the way to the bottom. The error here is that there may not be enough evidence to prove that the first event will lead to a chain reaction and cause the result claimed. Each step in the process would have to be examined carefully to be certain it would lead to the next step all the way to the end result, the claimed conclusion. You can easily see in the next example that it is possible that each event will not lead to the next. Example: If your dog begs for treats, you will always give it treats, and because you always give it treats, your dog will become fat and a fat dog does not live long, so your dog will die before it gets old. Since the chain of events could be changed or halted at any given point, it is a fallacious argument that if your dog begs for treats, your dog will die before it gets old. Rest assured that your dog does not have to fall victim to this slippery slope even if it begs for treats.

Weak Analogy

An analogy is a comparison between two things. A strong analogy finds likenesses that help us to understand one of the two things accurately. A weak analogy is misleading and results in a poorer understanding or a weak argument for any conclusion based on the weak analogy. Does it make sense to say "Fences are like jails and take away people's freedom, so fences should be outlawed." The analogy between the fence and the jail is weak, and therefore, the argument is weak. Even though we might be able to agree that in some situations fences are like jails, the conclusion is not logical because not all fences are like jails, and it is possible that very few fences are like jails. Furthermore, even though all fences may take away a degree of peoples' freedom, there are good reasons for this, and the degree to which people's freedom is taken away is not nearly as drastic as a jail. Finally, unlimited freedom is neither safe nor sensible even when certain freedoms are guaranteed in a society. Using a weak analogy weakens the argument being made. Free thinkers will look for solidly strong arguments and consider the whole picture before being convinced.

False Dichotomy/Either-Or Argument

When an argument presents only two possibilities but other possibilities exist it is called a false dichotomy. You may also hear it called an either-or argument. It would lead you to believe there are only two choices. By hiding or not recognizing the other possible choices, a person can present what sounds like a strong argument but is really a propagandistic ploy. Such an effort can sway the citizen caught off guard. Free thinkers will look for and consider all possibilities before being convinced. Many arguments for war have been made using false dichotomy. Here are a few. 1.) Americans must fight and beat the North Vietnamese or Communism will spread throughout the world. 2.) Either we invade Iraq or their leader will attack us with weapons of mass destruction. 3.) Either we bomb first, or we will be bombed. The either-or argument is often illogical. Look for other possibilities and consider all possibilities before deciding the course of action you support.

Straw Man Fallacy

The straw man argument is truly dishonest and underhanded. It presents a watered-down version of a logical argument and then shows why the argument is weak. It's easy to show weakness in an argument if you reduce the strong version of the argument to simplistic talking points, a habit of many politicians and political groups. Free-thinking people will demand the opportunity to consider and evaluate all arguments based on the entire version and its merits and not on an opponents' version of an argument. Unfortunately, our contemporary mindset is that we can understand an issue or argument by listening to a speech, tweet, or news broadcast. It doesn't happen that way. Important issues require serious consideration and attention to the details of the issue. This takes free thinking, time, and work to inform oneself. Almost always you will need to consider thoughtfully several sides of the issue. Never expect a politician to give you a complete version of their opponents' arguments. Too frequently the politician will give only a straw man argument before tearing it apart.

Missing the Point Fallacy

With this fallacy conclusions are made that are not actually supported by the facts and reasoning given. One misses the point if his or her reasoning gets him or her to make the wrong conclusion. Here is an example. Chuck leaves dirty dishes in the kitchen all day. Chuck spends his morning hiking and much of his afternoon getting a suntan in his lounge chair, then he goes to the hot springs to soak and exercise. Conclusion: His wife thinks Chuck is a lazy person. Wait a minute. The conclusion is missing the point. Chuck's choice of how he spends his time does not truly indicate he is lazy. He gets his exercise and the heat of the hot springs is therapeutic. He considers sun-tanning one of the pleasures of retirement. The dishes will be done after dinner so that the minimum amount of precious daylight will be interrupted with this chore. Chuck believes he has his priorities in order, and the dishes can wait. Sometimes a conclusion will miss the point if we do not get enough information and facts before drawing a conclusion. Other times people simply draw conclusions that do not follow from the reasons given. Do not jump to conclusions too hastily, and always try to get the whole picture (all the facts and details) before drawing a conclusion. You don't want to be guilty of missing the point.

Begging the Question or Circular Reasoning

This fallacious argument can be difficult to detect. It is called circular reasoning because the conclusion is only a rephrasing of the premise, the belief or fact an argument is based upon. If you are simply repeating yourself using different words, you are not making a logical argument. Your reasons are not reasons. They are circling back to repeat the conclusion rather than leading and supporting the conclusion. Let's say you argue, "Active euthanasia is morally acceptable; therefore, it is a good thing to allow suffering people to choose a comfortable death." In this argument the reason is the same as the conclusion. Good and morally acceptable are the same, while death and euthanasia are the same. Essentially, there are no actual reasons given for the conclusion. The entire argument is one conclusion. How might a real argument for euthanasia look? Forcing people to suffer when relief is available through euthanasia is cruel. If freedom is an inalienable right, people should be free to choose how and when they want to die. There are many available methods of performing safe and painless euthanasia. Therefore, it is a good thing to allow suffering people to choose a comfortable death. In this latter argument there are 3 reasons that lead to the conclusion: 1. It is cruel to make people suffer. 2. Freedom is an inalienable right, and 3. Painless and safe methods of euthanasia are numerous and available.

Another form of begging the question fallacy is to ignore an incorrect or questionable assumption upon which the argument is based. Here is an example: "Birth control allows men and women to be promiscuous. Sexual promiscuity is immoral. Therefore, birth control is immoral." In this example the assumption being left out is "Using birth control always leads to sexual promiscuity." It begs or evades the question "Does using birth control <u>always</u> lead to sexual promiscuity." By ignoring this important assumption, the argument sounds good, but is not good. To be a strong argument, all assumptions that form the basis of the argument must be made clear. One can see how very hard it is to recognize when an important assumption is being left out. What is not there is difficult to notice.

When evaluating an argument, try writing down all the reasons given for the conclusion. Next, identify assumptions made that have not been clearly stated. Finally, delete reasons that are simply a rephrasing of the conclusion. Now, evaluate. Is the argument strong? Are all parts of the argument true and factual? Are opinions that can be disputed weakening the argument? Does the argument beg the question or engage in circular reasoning?

Red Herring Fallacy

The Red Herring fallacy is actually no argument at all. Instead, it is the use of distraction to avoid the argument. To use it a person would first try to get on the upside of an argument and then deftly switch the subject in an attempt to turn the conversation away from the argument. For example, if arguing the merits of a proposed budget, a politician might begin to talk about the fact that his opponent supported a tax hike in the last session of Congress. What his opponent supported previously has nothing to do with the merits of the current budget proposal. It is simply a distraction—a red herring. If it succeeds, the politician will not have to continue to argue the merits of the budget he may be supporting. The audience may let him off the hook for a budget proposal that is unsatisfactory. If you recognize you are being thrown a red herring distraction, it is fair to interject a question or comment that brings people back to the issue of concern. In fact, others will thank you for it.

Equivocation

This fallacy uses words that have more than one meaning (homonyms) in an argument that does not make sense based on the actual meaning of the words, but the argument may sound sensible because the words are the same. Check this out. The new tax plan raises a fair amount of money for Medicare and Medicaid. Therefore, the new tax plan is fair to everybody. The repetition of the word fair in both the reason and the conclusion may make this sound good enough, but it does not make it logical. Here's a question for those of you that like challenging your free-thinking logic: If something is the right thing to do, does it mean you have a right to do it? Mmm…I can certainly see situations where you might not have a right to do what seems to be the right thing. Take euthanasia. It may seem like the right thing in certain circumstances, yet in most states it is not considered a right for anyone. In those states that allow euthanasia it is highly regulated and only licensed professionals have the right to perform it for another person. Equivocation is a sly argumentative trick like the slight-of-hand in a card trick.

Appeal to Pity

Some people will try to convince you to draw their conclusions about an issue based on pity. Many charities request your money using this technique as their sole argument. This is unfortunate because there are almost always other good arguments that can be given. However, humans are moved by their emotions, and as we indicated in Chapter 1, logical reasoning can often be outweighed by emotion. In the case of charity this may not be bad, but in the case of business and political decisions this could be catastrophic. If you feel your heartstrings being plucked in the political arena, see if you can write down the logical reasons behind the conclusion tearing at your heart. This will help you prevent being swayed by an appeal to pity.

Appeal to Ignorance

This argument asks you to accept someone's conclusion because there is a lack of evidence to conclude otherwise. Be wise. Lack of evidence is not an argument; it is simply a lack of evidence. If no evidence is available, the appropriate response is to look for evidence by authorizing and funding some research. Blindly accepting a conclusion based on nothing is a fool's errand.

Fallacies Used as Propaganda

Hasty Generalization Fallacy

This fallacy is related to the Glittering Generalities propaganda technique explained in Chapter 3. When we make a generalization, we are assuming that "all are the same." When we make assumptions about a whole group or range of cases based on a sample that is too small, our hasty generalization is often wrong. Stereotypes of people are a form of this fallacy. Not all librarians are shy and smart; not all rich people are snobs; not all religious people are narrow-minded, etc. Be skeptical if someone attempts to convince you that "Something or someone is *always* a certain way." Hasty generalizations, like stereotypes, are very often untrue but are often and easily used as propaganda.

Appeal to Authority Fallacy

Just as using a famous person to sponsor a product really says nothing about the truth of the product, appealing to a famous person's opinion about an issue is not a real argument for one side or the other on that issue. If an authority figure lends only his or her name to a cause but not a logical argument for that cause, then the appeal to authority is fallacious and should be ignored. Experts should be listened to when they offer reasoned arguments and facts, but not when all they give is their credentials or fame.

Ad Populum/Bandwagon Fallacy

Because everybody believes it, does it, thinks it, etc. is no proof it is good, better, or true. The bandwagon propaganda technique is sometimes used as part of an argument, but it is a weak non-argument. It is of no value when looking for logical reasons to evaluate an argument or issue. My personal feeling when I hear someone argue, "Well, many people believe (say, think, etc.)…" is that this person sure sounds stupid to suggest something should be believed just because others believe it. This is just like the "Jumping Off the Bridge" saying. Just because everyone else is doing it, doesn't mean it is a smart thing to do.

Bad Person/Hypocrite Fallacy

It has only been in our 2016 national election that calling an opponent a bad person and vilifying him or her became a pattern among some politicians. It is dishonorable, a form of propaganda, and it has nothing to do with the issues and arguments voters should be paying attention to. We do want and need people of good character in leadership positions, and we should certainly try to determine the facts regarding the character of those we wish to represent us. However, it should be a dead give-away when an opponent tries to vilify his or her opposition that the person vilifying is throwing a gut punch instead of arguing the merits of his or her own ideas. It is a dishonorable way to try to win an argument and reflects poorly on the person's character using such fallacy. Fair play does not include smearing an opponent's character. Let the facts inform our free-thinking opinions of a person's character.

Summary

Just like propaganda, when you combine fallacious argument with our own confirmation bias, free thinking may turn up dead. Don't let this happen to you. Take the time to think about what is being presented as logical. Analyze it by looking at each part carefully to make sure it is actually logical. Remember that when we are caught up in a crowd, herd instinct may creep into our emotional reactions. Escape the herd and take some time to let your free thinking evaluate the arguments and the logic behind whatever has been presented. Come to your own conclusions using your values and your thinking skills.

CONCLUSION

These are the times that try men's souls. The summer soldier and the sunshine patriot will, in this crisis, shrink from the service of their country; but he that stands by it now, deserves the love and thanks of man and woman. Tyranny, like hell, is not easily conquered; yet we have this consolation with us. That the harder the conflict, the more glorious the triumph. What we obtain too cheap, we esteem too lightly; it is dearness only that gives every thing its value.

--Thomas Paine, "The Crisis"
1776

Many people simply turn off the social and political turbulence and choose to live in their comfort zone. I urge my countrymen to be winter soldiers and cloud-cover patriots. It is when we let our guard down and believe that our democracy will be served well enough by others that corruption can take root. Many countries have tried to hold onto democracy but have been defeated by corruption. We must always be vigilant. We must not shrink from the service of our country. The greatest service we can give is the deliberate and consistent exercise of our free thinking. For it is in the voting booth where we will protect our democracy; and our voting must be free of the coercion perpetrated by propaganda, fallacy, fictional news, and confirmation bias. Democracy is not just a political system. Democracy is a way of life. To this end, I hope this handbook will serve its purpose in the readers' lives.

In his *Farewell Address*, George Washington cautioned Americans against forming factions and giving way to the party spirit. The reason he gave this caution was due to the negative effects which the partisan spirit kindles in society:

"[Partisanship] serves always to distract the public councils and enfeeble the public administration. It agitates the community with ill-founded jealousies and false alarms, kindles the animosity of one part against another, foments occasionally riot and insurrection. It opens the door to foreign influence and corruption, which finds a facilitated access to the government itself through the channels of party passions. Thus, the policy and the will of one country are subjected to the policy and will of another."

--George Washington

We are fortunate to have been given the wisdom of George Washington. His words and his deeds not only saved our country from tyranny, but from the self-destruction that might have prevented these United States from uniting. We would do well to heed his counsel today. It is clear that political parties have become detrimental tribes in our country. This situation has arisen from the unwillingness to exercise our free thinking to overcome herd instinct. We must fix this before it destroys us, and we must recognize that no politician, pastor, or person other than ourselves can fix it for us. Each citizen has the responsibility to contribute his or her free thinking. The very definition of democracy implies that free thinking is our duty.

We, you and I, are the keepers of our democracy.

Reference Notes

1. McLeod, S.A. *Simply Psychology*. (2017) "Maslow's hierarchy of needs". Accessed 10 October 2017. www.simplypsychology.org/maslow.html.
2. Ibid.
3. Ibid.
4. Ibid.
5. Gore, Al. *The Assault on Reason.* New York: The Penguin Press, 2007. p.73.
6. Ibid.
7. Azarian, Bobby, PH.D. *Mind in the Machine*. 31 December 2016. "Fear and Anxiety Drive Conservatives' Political Attitudes". Psychology Today. Accessed 23 February 2018. https://www.psychologytoday.com/blog/mind-in-the-machine/201612/fear-and-anxiety-drive-conservatives-political-attitudes.
8. Haidt, Jonathan. *The Righteous Mind: Why good people are divided by politics and religion*. New York: Vintage Books, 2012.
9. Ibid.
10. Shermer, Michael. *The Believing Brain*. New York: Times Books, 2011.
11. Brooks, David. *NYTimes.com*. "The Siege Mentality Problem." *The New York Times* 13 November 2017. Accessed 28 December 2017. https://www.nytimes.com/2017/11/13/opinion/roy-moore-conservative-evangelicals.html.
12. Ibid.
13. Ibid.
14. Ibid.
15. Harrison, Guy P. *Think Before You Like*. Amherst, New York: Prometheus Books, 2017.
16. Glen Beck: 'We have to start looking to heal'. *Reliable Sources*. 25 February 2018. https://www.cnn.com/videos/tv/2018/02/25/glenn-beck-we-have-to-start-looking-to-heal-rs.cnn/video/playlists/reliable-sources-highlights/
17. Harrison, Guy P. *Think Before You Like*. Amherst, New York: Prometheus Books, 2017.
18. Woolley, S.C. and Howard, P.N. *Computational Propaganda Research Project Working Paper No. 2017.11.* Oxford, UK: Project on Computational Propaganda. Undated. http://blogs.oii.ox.ac.uk/politicalbots/wpcontent/uploads/sites/89/2017/06/Casestudies-ExecutiveSummary.pdf Accessed 21 August 2018.
19. Tamir, D.I. and J.P. Miller. *Proceedings of the National Academy of Sciences of the United States of America*. "Disclosing Information About Yourself is Intrinsically Rewarding." May 2012. National Academy of Sciences. Accessed 25 February 2018. http://www.pnas.org/content/109/21/8038.
20. Ritvo, M.D., Eva. "Facebook and Your Brain." 24 May 2012. *Psychology Today*. Accessed 25, February 2018. https://www.psychologytoday.com/blog/vitality/201205/facebook-and-your-brain.
21. Baraniuk, Chris. "World Wide Warp." *New Scientist*. 20 February 2016. P.38
22. Steinmetz, Katy. "The Real Fake News Crisis: Bots and Propagandists are Just Part of the Problem. The Bigger Issue is Your Brain." *TIME*. 26 August 2018. Pp. 26-31.

23. LaFrance, Adrienne. "The Internet is Mostly Bots." *The Atlantic*. 31 January 2017. Accessed 26 February 2018. https://www.theatlantic.com/technology/archive/2017/01/bots-bots-bots/515043/

24. Zeifman, Igal. "Bot Traffic Report 2016." 24 January 2017. *ImpervaINCAPSULA*. Accessed 26 February. https://www.incapsula.com/blog/bot-traffic-report-2016.html.

25. Watts, Clint. *Messing with the Enemy: Surviving in a Social Media World of Hackers, Terrorists, Russians, and Fake News*. New York, NY: Harper Collins Publishers, 2018. p. 79-84.

26. Shaffer, Kris and Bill Fitzgerald. "Spot a Bot: Identifying Automation and Disinformation on Social Media." 5 June 2017. *Medium.com/ Data for Democracy*. Accessed 21 January 2018. https://medium.com/data-for-democracy/spot-a-bot-identifying-automation-and-disinformation-on-social-media-2966ad93a203.

27. Rather, Dan and Elliot Kirschner. *What Unites Us*. Chapel Hill, NC: Algonquin Books of Chapel Hill, 2017.

28. Popken, Ben. "Russian Trolls Duped Global Media and Nearly 40 Celebrities." NBCNews.com. 4 November 2017. NBC News Digital. Accessed 28 February 2018. https://www.nbcnews.com/tech/social-media/trump-other-politicians-celebs-shared-boosted-russian-troll-tweets-n817036

29. Moeller, Susan D. "Social Media and Foreign Policy." *Great Decisions 2018 Edition*. 26 November 2017. p.49.

30. Confessore, Nicholas and Daisuke Wakabayashi. "How Russia Harvested American Rage to Reshape U.S. Politics." *NYTimes.com*. 9 October 2017. *The New York York Times* Company. Accessed 1 March 2018. https://www.nytimes.com/2017/10/09/technology/russia-election-facebook-ads-rage.html

31. *MediaBiasFactCheck.org*. "Questionable Sources." Undated. Accessed 2 March 2018. https://mediabiasfactcheck.com/fake-news/

32. *The Writing Center*. 2018. University of North Carolina at Chapel Hill. Accessed 22 March 2018. https://writingcenter.unc.edu/tips-and-tools/fallacies/

Works Consulted & Suggested Reading

Non-Fiction

The Computational Propaganda Project: Algorithms, Automation and Digital Politics. Oxford Internet Institute. University of Oxford. www.comprop.oii.ox.ac.uk/

MediaBiasFactCheck.org. "Questionable Sources." Undated. Accessed 2 March 2018. https://mediabiasfactcheck.com/fake-news/

Messing with the Enemy: Surviving in a Social Media World of Hackers, Terrorists, Russians, and Fake News by Clint Watts
ISBN 978-0-06-279598-4
Copyright 2018

Think Before You Like: Social Media's Effect on the Brain and the tools You Need to Navigate Your Newsfeed by Guy P. Harrison
Copyright 2017

The Truth Matters by Bruce Bartlett
ISBN 978-0-399-58116-8, eBook ISBN 978-0-399-58117-5
Copyright 2017

The Righteous Mind by Jonathan Haidt
ISBN 978-0-307-45577-2
Copyright 2012

The Believing Brain by Michael Shermer
ISBN 978-0-8050-9125-0
Copyright 2011

The Assault on Reason by Al Gore
ISBN 978-1-59420-122-6
Copyright 2007

Fiction

1984 by George Orwell
ISBN-13: 9780451524935
Copyright 1949 renewed 1977

Fahrenheit 451 by Ray Bradbury
ISBN 978-1-9821-0260-9, eBook ISBN 978-1-4391-4267-7
Copyright 1951 renewed 1995

Animal Farm by George Orwell
ISBN-13: 978-8129116123
Copyright 1945

Acknowledgements

As with any endeavor to write and publish a book, there are many people who have been supportive and helpful. I am indebted to my husband for having patience when he really wanted me to go with him to the hot springs, but I wanted to work on the book.

I am also indebted to the help of those who have reviewed the manuscript and given the painful feedback that it still needs work. I am very indebted to Darcy McDaniel for her suggestions on content and to Linn Wallace for his editorial expertise.

I am also very grateful to friends and family who endured my prodding for feedback and gave it. And, of course, a huge thank you must be given to all those listed in references who did much of the research and have the expertise that supported this effort. I hope you will thank them as well by reading the books listed in "Works Consulted & Suggested Reading" that have inspired and informed this handbook.

Finally, a big shout out to you the reader. Thank you for your desire to think freely and exert your freedom and independence from the powerful and manipulative forces we all face. It is your desire and effort to do so that will allow my book to bear fruit. My very best wishes as you endeavor to exert your brainpower and achieve your freedom of thought.

The Author

www.ingramcontent.com/pod-product-compliance
Lightning Source LLC
Chambersburg PA
CBHW072256260726
48658CB00001BA/259